ERIN ACHANE • JACQUELYN JONES
RON CAMPBELL • PRISCILLA JONES

Kingdom Camouflaged:

8 Voices, 1 Mission: Fighting Back Against Scripture Distorted by Culture

JOHN DAVIDSON JR. • JEANETTE LEBRON
PATSY HILL • HERBERT POOLE

Produced for Publication by The Author's Pen, LLC
PO Box 16381
Fort Worth, Texas 76132
www.tapwriting.com

Kingdom Camouflaged/

Erin Achane; Jacquelyn Jones; Ron Campbell; Priscilla Jones;
John Davidson Jr.; Jeanette Lebron; Patsy Hill; Herbert Poole.

-- 1st printed. ISBN 978-1-948248-67-9.

Dedication

This book is dedicated to Pastor Bonne' Moon-Johnson, Bishop T.D. Jakes, our Director, Pastor Patrick Winfield II, the elders, teachers, teacher assistants, ministers, and administrative personnel at The Potter's House School of Ministry.

Our lives are forever changed because of your obedience and sacrifice. As the class of 2024 graduates, we represent the fruit sprouting from the seeds you have planted.

"I have planted, Apollos watered; but God gave the increase."
—1 Corinthians 3:6 KJV

Acknowledgments

First and foremost, we give all glory and honor to God, the Author and Finisher of our faith. Without His grace, vision, and relentless love, this book would not exist.

To our beloved families: thank you for your unwavering support, patient understanding, and endless prayers. Your encouragement in the quiet moments, your sacrifices in the background, and your love in every season have been the steady foundation beneath our journey. You've helped us stand when we felt like falling, and your belief in this calling strengthened our resolve to keep going.

To our friends, our chosen family: thank you for showing up, cheering us on, and speaking life to us when we doubted ourselves. Your emotional support, your messages, meals, and moments of celebration have been deeply felt and eternally cherished.

To our co-authors and contributing voices: what a divine honor to link arms with you in this Kingdom assignment. Each of you brought more than words; you brought your warfare, your wisdom, and your worship. Your vulnerability, obedience, and depth have added layers of glory to these pages. Thank you for your yes. Thank you for standing on the Kingdom.

To those who labored beside us behind the scenes—our editors, designers, mentors, intercessors, and The Author's Pen (for keeping it real with us)—your excellence and anointing did not go unnoticed. You were sent by God for this moment.

And finally, to you, the reader who picks up this book with a heart open to encounter Jesus, we acknowledge you. This was written with you in mind. May the truths within draw you deeper into purpose, healing, and holy fire, empowering you to embrace the journey ahead.

With deepest gratitude.

Foreword by Cora B. Jakes

The moment I laid eyes on the title Kingdom Camouflaged, my spirit leapt. I knew immediately that this was more than just a book it was a clarion call to the remnant, a spiritual wake-up alarm to Believers who have been lulled into complacency by a culture that has blurred the lines between Scripture and slogans. And who better to sound that alarm than eight bold ministers on fire, fresh out of the Potter's House School of Ministry, who aren't afraid to declare what thus says the Lord?

As I read these pages, I could feel the chains breaking. Not because of poetic language or cute captions, but because of the truth. And it reminded me of a line I wrote in Ferocious Warrior: "You cannot fight a spiritual battle with fleshly weapons." This book doesn't just equip you with truth it arms you with spiritual weapons. And as I always say in Faithing It, "Faith is the key to unlocking the power of God in your life." This book is filled with faith. It confronts distortion with discernment, and it reminds you that the Word is not just inspiration it's instruction.

We are living in a time where deception is celebrated, where emotionalism is mistaken for anointing, and where compromise has become currency. But God is raising a standard. He is calling us back to our roots, back to the Word, back to our spiritual identity. And this book? It's part of that call.

Each chapter confronts a phrase that has slipped into our churches, our homes, and even our theology, and gently but firmly calls it back into divine order. That's what Kingdom work is. It's not always glamorous. It's not always liked. But it's always needed. And the truth is, we don't need more viral quotes we need more biblical clarity. We need more spiritual accountability. We need more people willing to tear down every high thing that tries to exalt itself above the knowledge of God.

This is not the season to play Church. This is the season to be the Church. To stand in righteousness. To war in the Spirit. To teach with boldness. To pray with fire. To preach with conviction. And to live with integrity. What I love about this book is that it holds no punches. It is not interested in being popular it is committed to being prophetic. The ministers who poured into this book did just that. I salute them. I honor their obedience. And I echo their mission. They are not just writers; they are warriors. And their pens have become weapons.

Because I too have seen how the enemy loves to twist truth. I've lived through the war between what sounds good and what is good. I've watched culture seduce the Church into silence. But I've also watched God raise up a remnant people who don't care about being politically correct, but spiritually convicted. People who understand that deliverance doesn't come through likes and shares it comes through obedience and surrender. This book is for them. And this foreword is for you.

To the reader: let me tell you right now this won't be an easy read. But it will be a necessary one. You will be challenged. You may be offended. But if you stick with it, you will be changed. And that's the point. Transformation doesn't happen in your comfort zone. It happens when the Holy Spirit wrecks everything you thought you knew and rebuilds you in truth. It happens when we stop performing for the world and start posturing ourselves before the throne.

In Ferocious Warrior, I said, "There is a warrior within you that hell is terrified of." I believe this book will awaken that warrior. I believe it will help you put down culture's camouflage and pick up Kingdom authority. I believe it will call you into deeper accountability and greater alignment. When I wrote Faithing It, I was writing to the wounded, the overlooked, the tired, and the hungry. And I still am. This book is a mirror and a map. It shows you where you've been deceived and points you back to the truth.

So as you turn these pages, turn your heart toward God. Be open. Be teachable. Be willing to be stretched. Ask God to search you, convict you, and lead you. Ask Him to show you the lies you've believed, the slogans you've embraced, and the parts of you that still need deliverance.

Because God is still speaking. And He's using these authors to do it. So, turn off the noise. Silence the static. Pick up your sword. And remember who you are. You are a chain breaker. You are a warrior. You are a Kingdom citizen.

I'll leave you with this: When you start faithing it, you stop faking it. You start walking in purpose. You start walking in power. You start breaking chains.

Welcome to the war. Let's win it together.

—Cora B. Jakes

Table of Contents

Introduction

In this book, our mission is simple: **to make it plain.**

As new graduates, we bring a fresh perspective to the Word of God. We are not your average ministers, and we are not your average authors.

God has entrusted us with a special mission. As ministers chosen for this moment, this season, this shift, and this movement, we have been called upon to use our collective past and unwavering faith to release a sound that will pierce through your natural senses and awaken your Spirit.

We're not here to impress you. We're here to ignite something within you. We are delving into popular quotes and trendy phrases that have been passed around so often that they've lost their original weight. Phrases that started out holy, but somewhere along the way, got watered down into cute slogans hanging on bedroom walls.

It's time to put some respect back on His name. The name that is above all names. The King of Kings and the Lord of Lords. The Alpha and the Omega. The Great I Am.

While we have more money, technology, access, and freedom than our grandparents ever dreamed of, we are more depressed, more distracted, and we lack real discernment and power. Our grandparents *knew* God. We know reels, speakers, and conferences. We grew up *going* to church. Now, our kids are growing up quoting memes and thinking the Bible says, "Only God can judge me." That's not in the Old or New Testament, that's Tupac Shakur.

We see people praying to *"the Universe"* — you're close, but you must go deeper. You don't have to wait for the universe to align the stars with Venus to get your miracle. The Universe was created by God.

"The earth was without form, and void; and darkness was on the face of the deep. And the Spirit of God was hovering over the face of the waters."
—Genesis 1:2 NKJV

We love "#goodvibes" and talk about "protecting our energy." And you're so close, but you must go higher to receive this. Why is it so hard to make it make sense?

"Be sober-minded; be watchful. Your adversary the devil prowls around like a roaring lion, seeking someone to devour."
—1 Peter 5:8 ESV

Let's be clear, Satan is your real *Opp.*[1]

We recognize what an Opp looks like in the streets, but too many of us have forgotten who the real Opp is in the Spirit.

Your real enemy is not your ex, your boss, or your hater—it's Satan.

This book was born out of a deep conviction. Too many Believers, and even whole churches, are speaking things that

1 "Opp," short for opposition, your enemy, your rival, or your hater.

sound good, feel right, and go viral on social media, but aren't rooted in the Word of God.

We've been repeating phrases without real power.

We've been reposting captions without real understanding.

We've been quoting culture more than Christ.

And behind it all, your true Opp—Satan—has been loving every minute of it.

Let's tell it like it is:

The Kingdom has been camouflaged.

Culture has dressed it up, covered it over, and tried to rewrite its authority.

The values of heaven have been buried under hashtags, horoscopes, and half-truths.

Culture has redefined righteousness, rebranded rebellion, and renamed sin to make it palatable.

But let's be clear:

The Kingdom of God will not be rewritten. It will not bow to trends. It will not be mocked.

"Heaven and earth will pass away, but My words will by no means pass away."
—Matthew 24:35 NKJV

The Kingdom of God will stand forever.

Today, we fight back.

This is more than a book; this is a weapon for your mouth, your mind, and your mission.

Inside these pages, you'll find thirteen chapters, each one confronting a common phrase we hear in Christian spaces — and bringing it back under the authority of Scripture.

Eight authors. One voice. One mission:

To expose the real Opp and equip you to walk in Kingdom truth.

We didn't come to play.

We came to tell the truth.

We came to set captives free.

We came to remind the world:

"For we wrestle not against flesh and blood, but against principalities, against powers, against the rulers of the darkness of this world, against spiritual wickedness in high places."
—Ephesians 6:12 KJV

The real battle isn't against people—it's against the enemy of your soul.

If you're tired of empty words,

If you're tired of fighting the wrong fights,

If you're ready to stop giving Satan a pass —

If you're ready to stand on the Word and fight the right fight —

Turn the page. The war over your faith starts now.

CHAPTER 1

You Cannot Serve Two Masters

By: Minister Erin Achane

"No one can serve two masters. Either you will hate the one and love the other, or you will be devoted to the one and despise the other. You cannot serve both God and money."
—Matthew 6:24 NIV

When I got my first job at the age of sixteen at Mr. Gatti's Pizza and started to miss church to make some extra money on Sundays, my grandmother used to tell me, "You can't serve two masters." My grandmother was warning me early that you can't serve God and money at the same time with your whole heart. Eventually, one's gone get pushed to the side. At the time, I thought she was simply being a grandmother, always telling me things that made no sense. Later, I realized she was laying the foundation that would lead me to the ultimate decision to choose God over everything else, even money.

To serve, in Greek, is the word *douleuo,* which means to be a slave to, to be in bondage, to be fully subject to a master. It means to be completely devoted to. Jesus is explaining how eventually you will grow more in love with one master and hate the other. This happens so gradually that it can be hard to catch. We pray for the job, and God answers our prayers. We get the job with the fat paycheck and the grand office with the huge window. We can finally pay our bills, take care of our families, and save for a rainy day. It always starts out with the best intentions. But when we serve Mammon, over time, money becomes the mission. It's all the Benjamins, baby! We start to filter our decisions, our identity, and our trust through the lens of "How will this affect my money?" We take a job, move to another city, or choose our future spouse because it will line our pockets, and not because it aligns with our calling.

We start to measure who we are based on how much money is in our bank accounts, our job titles, or what type of car we drive. We start to feel important when we get a little money in the bank, and we feel worthless when we're broke. We start making decisions based on how it will make us look, instead of conviction. We start to base our value on material things instead of trusting in who God says we are. The world may measure your worth based on what they see on Instagram and Facebook, but God says in Ephesians 2:10:

"For we are God's masterpiece. He has created us anew in Christ Jesus, so we can do the good things he planned for us long ago."
—Ephesians 2:10 NLT

The struggle is real. God and money can represent two competing kingdoms, fighting for your allegiance. These two masters pull in two opposite directions. It's a battle over your mind. Mammon will tell you, "Don't trust God. He moves too slow. What if you lose everything?" When you make more money, then you will be happy and secure. We worship and praise God on Sunday, then lose sleep over bills Monday through Saturday. While God is telling you through His Word, "Put your trust in me! I am your provider; I am your protector."

Philippians 4:19 (NIV) says:
"And my God will meet all your needs according to the riches of his glory in Christ Jesus."

How might we quantify *his riches in glory* as it relates to money?

Haggai 2:8 (NIV), "The silver is mine and the gold is mine,' declares the Lord Almighty." It all belongs to God! When we start chasing God, money will chase us! In Deuteronomy 28, God has a laundry list of blessings he has promised us when we serve him. He says everything you touch will be blessed! Meanwhile, money is out here making promises it can't keep. Mammon thrives when our mindset is set on self-dependence, materialism, power, and control. It's fake news! None of it will last; we see it even today. Jobs that were considered "untouchable" are all at risk of becoming obsolete due to AI and machines. Federal and state jobs that were single-handedly the most secure jobs in the nation are gone with a stroke of a pen. Safety nets and protections for the poor, underserved, and elderly are no longer protected and are in serious jeopardy of ending with my generation.

God is showing all of us in real time that whatever is not built on His Word will not stand. Jesus uses money in this text, but it follows a theme throughout the Scripture. God wants us to surrender or give up serving ourselves and serve Him and Him alone. We must lay aside every weight and the sin that so easily beset us, according to Hebrews 12:1, and go boldly to his throne of grace, anticipating love and forgiveness. We must remember that if God's eyes are on the sparrows, how much more does He care and watch over us? We must remember that we are good wheat! (Matthew 13: 24-30 NKJV)

This parable was an aha moment in my walk with Jesus. It explained this spiritual battle in the *Parable of the Wheat and Tares*. God planted good wheat; that wheat is us. If you go to Genesis 1:26-31, God made us in His own image and gave us dominion. He saw everything he had made and said, Behold, it was good. So what happened to us? The enemy sowed weeds among it. The weeds are sin. God gave Adam and Eve instructions and gave them the ability to choose whether they would follow. They chose to disobey God. They made the choice, but Satan presented the opportunity. He lied to them and tempted them. I don't blame Adam and Eve. We don't wrestle with flesh and blood, remember. I blame Satan! So now, the wheat and the weeds must grow together until harvest. In the end, God will separate them on judgment day. The date is set, and He will separate the saved from the lost. When God created us, He made us good. But He did not create us to be robots that only do what he commands. He created us with the ability to choose which master we will serve.

If I can give it to you straight with no chaser, if you have not chosen to follow Jesus, you have already chosen the other guy by default. Trust and believe you are serving one of them. And if you don't know which one, I'll help you out; it's Satan. I know, I know. You are good wheat! But you still must choose Jesus and surrender to his authority.

We may wish there was an app out there we could download on our phone where we could click one button, but God doesn't work like our phone. He's old school for real! You can't order it on Uber Eats, you can't get it on Amazon Prime, and you can't stream it on Netflix. We must look inwardly at who we have become and examine how far we have shifted away from the presence of God. Our faith must be built on things eternal and not on things temporary. In order to grow our faith in Jesus, we first must humble ourselves and repent. Revelation requires that you get by yourself, step away from the phone very slowly, and ask the Lord to save you.

"If you declare with your mouth, 'Jesus is Lord,' and believe in your heart that God raised him from the dead, you will be saved."
—Romans 10:9 NIV

He wants us to repent. To admit we got it wrong, to admit we are not perfect, and go to Him with a sorrowful heart. The great news is He is waiting on you with open arms; He is ready to receive you.

"'Now, therefore,' says the Lord,
'Turn to Me with all your heart,
With fasting, with weeping, and with mourning.'
So rend your heart, and not your garments;
Return to the Lord your God,
For He is gracious and merciful,
Slow to anger, and of great kindness;
And He relents from doing harm."
—Joel 2:12-13 NKJV

He is sovereign. He is holy. He is faithful. He is the boss of the whole universe, and if you wanna be down, you have to choose him.

Now, to really break down the text, let's check its context. The text highlights that you cannot serve God and serve money.

In Matthew 6, Jesus is teaching on the mountain to a ton of people. He starts talking about money. He's telling the crowd not to store up their wealth on earth where other men can steal it, but instead store their riches in heaven. He says wherever your treasure is, that's where your heart will be also. Then, he says the lamp of your body is your eye. If your eye is good, your whole body will be full of light. If your eye is bad, then your whole body is full of darkness. What is Jesus saying? Your intentions, your motives, and your heart toward money need to be checked. The love of money is the root of all evil. Do you love money more than God?

If you try to serve both, eventually you will favor one and resent the other. The enemy figured this out with Adam and Eve. The gateway to sin is the lust of the eyes, wanting things that you see and don't have. Your eyes are the gateway to your heart and Satan uses visual temptation.

"For the weapons of our warfare are not carnal, but mighty through God to the pulling down of strong holds;
Casting down imaginations, and every high thing that exalteth itself against the knowledge of God, and bringing into captivity every thought to the obedience of Christ..."
—2 Corinthians 10:4-5 KJV

Don't let mammon be a high thing that exalts itself against the knowledge of God!

It's time to change the way we think about money. If you love God, you'll naturally begin to hate greed, pride, and self-reliance. If you love money, you'll begin to ignore, rationalize, or even unfriend what God's Word says about humility, giving, and sacrifice. When we serve only God as our master, we start to prioritize God over our money. When we get to that place, we see money as a tool to increase His Kingdom, not ourselves. And when we decrease, that's when he increases us!

Years ago, I was a member of an Assembly of God church in my hometown. When it was time for the offering, the pastor said something that shut up the voice that lived rent-free in my mind about titles. He said, "I am on salary. I get paid the same amount each month regardless of how much you give. So, I don't make more when you give more."

Something in me needed to hear that. We don't like to pay tithes because we don't want to give our money to the pastor so he can go get a new Mercedes while we have to put oil in our car every three days. I get it. But again, we are focused on the trees instead of the forest. Tithing isn't just about the church; it's about your heart. God wants to know if you trust Him. Malachi 3:10 (NIV): "'Bring the whole tithe into the storehouse, that there may be food in my house. Test me in this,' says the Lord Almighty, 'and see if I will not throw open the floodgates of heaven and pour out so much blessing that there will not be room enough to store it.'" We love to quote the end of that verse in church, but we ignore the beginning. Yet, the beginning of the Scripture is where God makes a bold statement. It is the only place in Scripture where God says, "Try me and find out!"

I would give about twenty bucks and feel like ok, That's good enough. God was increasing me according to my level of trust. Giving twenty dollars instead of my ten percent when I was earning $1,000.00 weekly meant I didn't trust God to meet my needs. I stayed broke. Something would always break. Since I did not trust God with my money in this season, the Lord started to show me the consequences of serving Mammon. My air conditioner would stop blowing cold air, my starter would go out, and I had a flat tire, all on the same day. It was so bad to the point where I would lose money! I was afraid to give my full ten percent, just in case of emergency, and I was in an "emergency" every week!

God put holes in my pocket!

One Sunday, I was sick of that mess. I paid my tithes with praise! Then, immediately after church, I started crashing out. Here comes the devil with his fear and doubt. "Girl, that was your bill money. What are you going to do?" I decided I would trust God. God knows I need my house. I had to believe he was going to make a way. And He did! After that, I couldn't stop paying my tithes. Everything I touched was increasing. He was blessing everything, not just my bank account but my Spirit. I started to trust him with more than just my money. I was developing a relationship with the Lord, and he was transforming my mind. The things I set as important started to fall off my to-do list, and His to-do list was becoming my ultimate goal. He started to show me, since I can trust you with money, here is some more!

For God to trust you with one million dollars, He must first trust you with a thousand. God will bless your money when it is not more important than Him.

> *"And it is impossible to please God without faith. Anyone who wants to come to him must believe that God exists and that he rewards those who sincerely seek him."*
> *—Hebrews 11:6 NLT*

This journey we've taken isn't just about money; it's about trust. It's about who your heart truly follows. Yes, Jesus spoke about money, but He was revealing something deeper: whatever you put above Him will eventually break you. Mammon isn't just cash; it's a spirit, a mindset, a silent master, and a terrible master. With Mammon, the house always wins, and you will eventually lose. But if you build your life on the rock, if you make that decision to accept Jesus as your Master and start to dismantle your current systems and rebuild on His word, His truth, and His character, you are building on a foundation that cannot be shaken. You are standing on the Kingdom of God! Choose to trust God, like in real life, not just with cheap words but with expensive actions. Surrender your heart, your money, your time, and your decisions to him, and watch everything begin to shift. When He becomes your main squeeze, and not your side chick, when you begin to do His word and not just repeat His Word, when you finally realize that you already have everything you need in Christ, you begin to function on such a high level of wealth and abundance not just in your bank account, but in your mind, your spirit, your relationships, your peace, and your purpose. You stop striving and start thriving because you're finally tapped into the source of all things.

CHAPTER 2
God IS Good!

By: Minister John Davidson Jr.

Finish this phrase:
"God is good all the time. And all the time_____".

You probably laughed or smiled while finishing that sentence. If you grew up in or around any church in America, especially in the South, chances are that you are very familiar with this phrase.

I grew up attending a Baptist church in New Orleans, Louisiana, where this phrase was repeated quite often. In this church, many older saints would say and repeat the phrase over and over. In fact, I don't think there was one Sunday that went by where I did not hear it multiple times. I believe it may have been frowned upon if you did not know the phrase. Everyone and their mother (and their mother's mother) said it. It was repeated so often that I naturally began to assume that it was some Bible verse.

"God is good all the time and all the time God is good!"

Now, I know I'm not the only one who thought this was Scripture. There are probably some of you reading this right now who still believe this phrase is a verse from the Word of God itself. However, it is not! The shocking truth is that no Scripture states these words. The phrase was just repeated so much in church culture by church people that we just adopted and accepted it as the written Word of God.

The actual factual is that this phrase was created by human beings who were more than likely using a verse from Psalms 100 as a source.

"For the LORD is good [God is good];
His mercy is everlasting [all the time]..."
—Psalms 100:5 KJV

Close enough, right? I mean, they're basically saying the same thing, right? Wrong! While the wording may be similar, the context is different. The context in which you read and use the Word of God is extremely important because context can change meaning. The context in which Psalms 100:5 is written is giving thanks to God. Thanks, because "...*He* [the Lord] *is good and His mercy is everlasting*...". In contrast, the context that we use(d) the phrase "God is good all the time..." was in a more general sense, to state that God is always good and never not. While this may be true, the generalization of the statement, sentiment, and mindset can be dangerous. Why? Because it can cause us to make some very erroneous assumptions about God that ignore the intricacies of His sovereignty. It can lead us to assume that since God is "always *good*," then He will always do good to us. Then, when we go through some things that we label as "*bad*," we will either misplace blame on the devil, or worse, blame God for not being "*good*" all the time. This would be a terrible error on our part because we would be giving misplaced credit/glory to the enemy of our souls (the devil) for the *bad* that we experience. Or even worse of an error would be to accuse the lover of our souls (God) of not being *good*.

The truth is that God **IS** good always and in all ways. God is eternally good! However, in His sovereignty and omnipotence, He does allow us to go through some *bad* for multiple reasons.

Sometimes it's to discipline us to help us get back onto the correct path.

"My child, don't reject the Lord's discipline, and don't be upset when He corrects you. 12For the Lord corrects those He loves, just as a father corrects a child in whom he delights."
—Proverbs 3:11-12 NLT

Sometimes, God allows *bad* to happen to us as consequences of our poor decisions, to keep us from repeating those poor decisions.

"Don't be misled you cannot mock the justice of God. You will always harvest what you plant."
—Galatians 6:7 NLT

Sometimes, God also uses *bad* to direct us onto our destiny path, which is the best path for our lives, or to steer us away from paths that are not meant for us (example: Saul *(who is also called "Paul")* on the road to Damascus).

Sometimes it's to show us and the world what we are truly made of so that God can get the glory through us (*example: Job*).

There are many reasons why God would allow us to go through some *"bad"* things in life. He is sovereign and omniscient (all-knowing). He has all understanding. His perspective and point of view is more vast, higher, and more dynamic than ours. As God explains in Isaiah 55:8-9 NLT:

> *"My thoughts are nothing like your thoughts," says the Lord. And my ways are far beyond anything you could imagine. For just as the heavens are higher than the earth, so my ways are higher than your ways and my thoughts higher than your thoughts."*

Therefore, we couldn't possibly begin to understand all of the reasons why God would allow *bad* to happen to us. However, we should still trust that God is eternally good, and just because He allows *bad* doesn't mean that He Himself is *bad*.

This may shock you, but God does sometimes use things that we consider "bad" as a tool to help us in our lives. Help to correct us, direct us, protect us from outside forces, and protect us from us.

For example, in ancient times (and in some parts of the world today), a farmer would use a goad to guide or encourage an animal to do something. A goad is a sharp or pointed stick to spur (poke) an animal, like oxen, to get them to go in a certain direction or keep them from going in the wrong direction.

Now, let's say that the farmer uses the goad to stop the ox from going in a direction that would get the ox seriously injured or even killed. To the ox, the goad-poke hurts, so it may think of the goad as *"bad"*. But to the farmer, the goad-poke directed the ox away from danger, which is a *"good"* thing. The farmer understands that a little pain now saved the ox from larger pain later. Therefore, we can say that the farmer used a *"bad"* thing for the overall *"good"* of the ox.

Understanding & Trust

The ox has to broaden his understanding and trust the farmer. Understand that the goad is not a part of the farmer, it's just a tool that the farmer uses. And trust that the farmer **is** good even though the tool he used did not *feel* good. It was good FOR the ox, but not good TO the ox.

We have to come to the same trust and understanding of God! We have to understand that the bad things God uses in our lives are NOT a part of Him; they are just tools that He uses for reasons that we may not be sure of at the moment. We also have to trust that **God is good**, even though some of the tools that He uses feel bad to us. It may feel bad TO us, but it is good FOR us.

Don't Get Stuck at Stuck!

We are better off going along with the 'goad-pokes' that God gives us instead of going against them. Just like Jesus told Saul/Paul on the road to Damascus in Acts 26:14 NKJV:

"And when we all had fallen to the ground, I heard a voice speaking to me and saying in the Hebrew language, 'Saul, Saul, why are you persecuting Me? It is hard for you to kick against the goads."

In other words, Jesus told Saul that it is hard for him [Saul] to go against Jesus' direction for his life. It's like kicking your bare foot against the sharp goad. It's hard to do continuously and you only cause yourself more pain. We only cause ourselves more pain and difficulty when we go against Jesus' direction and will for our lives.

We also can't let ourselves get stuck at 'goad-poked'. Many times, we get stuck in the place where we were 'stuck' (*pun intended*). When God sticks us to direct us or protect us, we often stay stuck in the mindset of *"ouch, that hurts, God!"* not realizing that the little prick that God allowed us to experience saved us from larger pain or even death. If someone pokes me so I don't step into a pit or off a cliff, I would thank that person because they saved me from destruction. I wouldn't complain about the pain from the poke because the poke-pain is less than the pit-pain.

Preventative Cost < Repercussion Cost

A broken arm and leg hurt more than a little poke from a sharp stick. Preventative cost is always less than the repercussion cost! This means that it costs less to prevent something from happening than it does to pay the cost after the damage is done. The same way that changing your car oil regularly costs less than never changing the oil, only to have your car engine seize up, rendering the whole car and engine useless. An approximate $80 oil change twice per year versus tens of thousands of dollars for a new car every two years is incomparable.

For those of you who are trying to do the math in your head, the comparison is approximately $310 for two years of oil changes versus approximately $30,000-$40,000 every two years for a new car. Preventative cost is **always** less than the repercussion cost! Significantly less.

We don't thank God enough for what He protects us from through prevention because we're too stuck on the fact that we got *poked,* and it hurt. Don't get stuck at the point of *stuck*.

God, our Creator!

We must broaden our understanding of God's sovereignty. And that God is thee Creator and the source of creativity. Which means that He is the most creative One of all. And as the most creative One, God doesn't need the best materials to create something "good" and beautiful.

If someone told me that they were creative but could only create something beautiful using the best materials, I would seriously question that person's ability, capability, and creativity.

It's easy to create something "good" when you're using the best materials. The true test of creativity is in what you are able to create using less-than-desirable materials.

God displays His creative mastery by using *good* AND *bad* things to create incredibly beautiful things. To take it a step further, God shows the vastness of His creativity by creating *good* FROM *bad*. Bringing out *beauty* from *the ugly*. And to take it even further, God shows His eternal omnipotence of creativity by His ability to create something from absolutely nothing at all.

The creation of the world proves these truths. God spoke into *nothing* and *something* appeared, and it was GOOD! God then took dirt (*nothingness*) and breathed into it, and we came to life!

> *"And the Lord God formed man of the dust of the ground, and breathed into his nostrils the breath of life; and man became a living being." —Genesis 2:7 NKJV*

After God created everything, He then reviewed it and saw that it was good. Indeed, it was very good!

Broken Understanding of *Good* and *Bad*

We have to understand that we have a broken understanding of "good" and "bad," which stems from our broken knowledge of good and evil. Yes, we have a broken knowledge of good and evil. We're not supposed to have it! That's why God told Adam and Eve not to eat of the "Tree of the Knowledge of Good and Evil" in the Garden of Eden.

Genesis 2:16-17 (NLT): "But the LORD God warned him, "You may freely eat the fruit of every tree in the garden except the tree of the knowledge of good and evil. If you eat its fruit, you are sure to die."

One of the side effects of the knowledge of good and evil is that we mislabel things and situations as either one or the other. Separate from God, we do not possess the eternal perspective necessary to go along with the knowledge to be able to judge/label something as good or evil. We don't have the perspective or vantage point to see a thing or situation start to finish, so we're not qualified to judge "good" or "bad". We need a higher perspective—God's perspective. And **only** God has that.

The closest thing that we get to that kind of perspective is hindsight, after we've gone through the whole thing in totality. Then, we can look back and properly assess whether the whole situation was good or bad. And even then, hindsight is not the same as the foresight, oversight, and insight that God has.

What I mean is, we live within time, so in many ways, we are trapped and confined to the parameters of time. Since we are "in it," we can't always see out of it. God exists in eternity. He always is, always was, and will always be The Great "I AM". Not "I was," "I will be," or "I'm becoming". No, He is The Great "I AM".

He's not trapped by the parameters of time. He has the higher seat, the higher perspective to see all of time at once. He can see things in totality, start to finish. He is the Author and Finisher. Alpha and Omega. The Beginning and End! So, He is truly qualified to judge something as actually good or evil because He sees the whole thing, the whole story, and the whole person.

Since we are in it, we can only see the thing, the story, the person for what they are at that specific moment in time. We don't see the whole, so we're not qualified to judge or label anything "good" or "evil".

Whole Story

Think about it like this: if you read a book that has one hundred chapters and five of those chapters seem *bad/negative,* and you decide to stop after reading one of those negative chapters and label the WHOLE book *"bad,"* then you've immaturely and prematurely judged/mislabeled that book.

If you were to read the whole book, you would know that the whole story isn't "bad"; it just had a few dark chapters. If you were to read the whole story, you might understand that the whole story might be beautiful, especially BECAUSE of those dark chapters.

We don't get that type of perspective—the proper perspective—until we finish the story. So, don't judge a book by its chapters. Don't judge your life by its chapters. Consider the whole story. Consider YOUR WHOLE story!

When we go through tough seasons in life, we immediately label our lives as "bad" because our perspectives are distorted by the pain and frustration of those dark chapters. Then, when we get through it, we see that it was for our good that we went through some "bad".

Like David explains in Psalms 119:65-68 and 71-72 NLT:

> 65 *You have done many good things for me, LORD, just as you promised.*
> 66 *I believe in your commands; now teach me good judgment and knowledge.*
> 67 *I used to wander off until you disciplined me; but now I closely follow your word.*
> 68 *You are good and do only good; teach me your decrees.*
>
> 71 *My suffering was good for me, for it taught me to pay attention to your decrees.*
> 72 *Your instructions are more valuable to me than millions in gold and silver.*

David said, "My suffering was <u>GOOD</u> for me!" Maybe not good TO me, but good FOR me.

So, let's stop prematurely mislabeling our tough seasons and situations in life and instead have a new perspective that God's ways are far beyond our ways, and He might be working something good *in* and *through* and *for* us. We just have to trust God and trust that He IS good all the time, and all the time He is good. Then, we can have hope while we patiently endure afflictions because we know it won't last *always,* like God's goodness.

Is God good? **Yes!**

Is God good all the time? **Yes!** God is good always and in ALL ways!

Should we *always* expect *good* from God? **No!**

Does God use bad things? **Yes!**

Does God use bad things for our ultimate good? **Yes!**

Can God take bad things and turn them good? **Yes!**

Can we trust God to always be good? **Yes!**

Can we trust God? **Yes!**

Can we ALWAYS trust God?! **Yes!!**

Can you though? Can you trust that God is still good even when you're going through something bad? Can you understand that what may be good FOR you may not be good TO you?

If so, then you are now ready to go to the next chapter (literally and figuratively).

CHAPTER 3

Though He Slay Me Yet Will I Trust Him

By: Minister John Davidson Jr.

"Why would you ever trust someone who has hurt you? That doesn't even make sense! How? How is it even possible? I could never!" These were some of the thoughts that I had as a youth whenever I heard the phrase: *"Though He slay me yet will I trust Him."*

People in church *(especially the older saints)* would repeat this phrase as an affirmation of faith for going through difficult times in life. Unlike many common church phrases, this one <u>is</u> Scripture. However, it's only part of the Scripture. We don't quote the whole verse in context.

In doing so *(not knowing the context)*, we leave doors open to make awful assumptions and accusations against God in that we falsely believe that He is responsible for *'slaying'* us. This is a horrible blame that we place on God. We know this is untrue based on what was discussed in the last chapter.

In the last chapter, we learned that *God <u>does</u> use things that don't feel good* ***to*** *us but are good* ***for*** *us*. And, *just because God uses something that we consider as 'bad' as a tool doesn't mean that the tool is a part of God's being*. God doesn't *slay us*! God doesn't use any part of His being to slay us. Instead, He uses His very being [Jesus] to give us life! Jesus says:

> *"The thief [Satan] does not come except to steal, and to kill, and to destroy. I have come that they may have life, and that they may have it more abundantly." —John 10:10 NKJV*

I wanted to make this point very early in this chapter to quickly dispel the misconception of God *'slaying us'* so we can spend the rest of the chapter exploring the deeper matters of what's hidden in the full context of our topic verse. Take a deep breath because we're going deep!

There is More

Quoting only part of a Bible verse without knowing the full context leaves us open to dangerous misunderstandings of both God and His Word. What is equally dangerous (*if not more so*) is what we miss out on when we quote partial Scripture. When we choose to quote, learn, or understand only part of a verse, we miss out on getting the full value of the verse. It's like taking a bite of an apple and then throwing the rest away. There is more there! There is more value that you can get out of that apple. Much more! The Word of God is the same. There is so much more value in the fullness of the Word of God versus just a piece of it taken out of context. And in the case of Job 13:15, we miss a colossal ton of value hidden within the text.

> *"Though He slay me, yet will I trust Him. Even so, I will defend my own ways before Him." —Job 13:15 NKJV*

This is the full verse. *"Even so, I will defend my own ways before Him"* is the part that we typically leave out. It doesn't appear to be much of a "miss" on the surface, but there is much more beneath the surface. What is the context in which Job is making this statement? What has led Job to make this intense statement? What are the circumstances leading up to this desperate declaration? What is Job's situation? What is Job's mindset and emotional state at this moment?

For better understanding, we'll explore further into Jobs' story of suffering. But first, we need some background story to set the scene.

A Conversation about Job

Job's story doesn't start with Job himself. In this way, Job's story is like many of ours. In fact, all of ours. All our stories don't begin with us. They begin with God! In Job's case, God is having a conversation with Satan about Job. Yes, God talks to Satan!

In this scene, Satan has gathered with the other spiritual beings who are members of the Heavenly court to give a report of their actions to the Lord God. God asks Satan where he has been, and Satan responds, "to and fro on the earth." Then, God suggests (*Yes, God suggests*) Job and brags about how blameless and upright Job is. Don't miss that! GOD BRAGS about Job in Heavenly courts!

> [9]*So Satan answered the LORD and said, "Does Job fear God for nothing?* [10]*"Have You not made a hedge [protection] around him, around his household, and around all that he has on every side? You have blessed the work of his hands, and his possessions have increased in the land.*

> [11]*"But now, stretch out Your hand and touch all that he has, and he will surely curse You to Your face!"*
> [12]*And the LORD said to Satan, "Behold, all that he has is in your power; only do not lay a hand on his person." So, Satan went out from the presence of the LORD. —Job 1:9-12 NKJV*

Let's pause for a few points of clarity.

1. The beginning of Job chapter one proves that the devil (Satan) **IS NOT** the opposite of God, nor does he have equivalent power to or ANY authority over God. He [Satan] is a creat*ed* being that is under the authority of thee Creator of all, and he [Satan] must report to and get permission from God, who is thee supreme authority over ALL! Amen? Amen!
2. Satan says to the Lord in verse 11, *"...stretch out YOUR HAND and touch all that he [Job] has."* God responds, *"Behold, all that he [Job] has is in YOUR power."* This reinforces the earlier point that God Himself is NOT the one who *'slays us.'* However, God may use tools (*even giving permission to or allowing evil as a tool*) for our overall good and for His eternal glory.
3. It was God who suggested Job to Satan, which means that Job's suffering was allowed by God AND initiated by God. This can be extremely difficult for us to understand because God's ways are so far beyond our ways. However, as we established in the last chapter, we CAN trust God!

Satan then leaves the presence of God, and indeed, destroys all that Job has. All of his possessions and even his children are killed and destroyed. Throughout all of this, Job doesn't sin, so Satan goes harder at Job. He [Satan] seeks (*and gets*) further permission from the Lord to attack Job's body. Job is then struck with painful boils from head to toe. The sequence and culmination of these horrific events send Job into a deep, dark downward spiral. And for us to uncover and discover the full value of the deeper truths buried within our core verse (Job 13:15), we must follow Job down this dark spiral. Take another deep breath. We're going even deeper!

Dread, Distress, Despair

At the moment when we see Job make his statement in verse 15, he has gone through some of the most unimaginable suffering, anguish, and loss. This is much more than "goad-poke" pain. (*See the last chapter*). We have graduated from *"Ouch, God, you poked me"* to *"My soul is crushed."* Job's suffering was compounded and multiplied. The fears that lurked in the deepest, darkest, hidden corners of Job's mind had become a reality. Dread had come!

> *"What I always feared has happened to me. What I dreaded has come true. I have no rest; only trouble comes."*
> *—Job 3:25-26 NLT*

Job's suffering is so great that he longs for death just so he can get some rest from the torment and the pain. Have you ever been to this place? This dark place of emotional, spiritual, and physical torment? Where the pain is so excruciating that you just want it to end by ANY means? Including death?! Job has sunk into that dark place of despair. And he wants to die just to get relief from the pain.

> *"If my misery could be weighed, and my troubles be put on the scales, they would outweigh all the sands of the sea."*
> *—Job 6:2-3 NLT*

"I wish He [God] would crush me. I wish He would reach out His hand and kill me. At least I can take comfort in this: Despite the pain, I have not denied the words of the Holy One."
—Job 6:9-10 NLT

Miserable Comforters

Death of his children. Loss of wealth and income. Loss of property. Loss of all dignity and respect. Body covered from head to toe in painful boils. No support from his spouse (*helper in life*)! Physically, emotionally, financially, mentally, and maritally broken! EVERYTHING except the breath in his lungs was taken away from Job. Life doesn't possibly get any worse than this! Does it?! Unfortunately, it does.

On top of everything that Job has to suffer in his moment of despair, Job's *friends,* who initially come to comfort him, eventually end up accusing him of sin, adding much insult to his open injuries. I call it '*in*salt', Like throwing salt into multiple open wounds that are torn open to the bone. This is pain that, on its own, is not as painful as the initial hurt, but the fact that the original hurt is so deep multiplies the sting of false accusations (*in*salts) exponentially.

Comfortless, Job is now left with the sting and burn of outrage and enrage.

They [*Job's friends*] were initially doing a good job of comforting him when they sat with him for seven days and were quiet (Job 2:11-13), but once they started to speak, they began to accuse Job of sinning and reaping the consequences of his sin. So much so that Job complained:

"One should be kind to a fainting friend, but you accuse me without any fear of the Almighty."
—Job 6:14 NLT

"Stop assuming my guilt, for I have done no wrong. Do you think I am lying? Don't I know the difference between right and wrong?"
—Job 6:29-30 NLT

Now, you know, I know, Job knew, and God knows that Job was not suffering because He had done something wrong or sinful. Job was suffering because God was pleased with Job and the way that he lived his life. God wanted to prove how blameless and upright Job was to Satan, to the Heavenly court, and to the whole world throughout eternity. Job was selected for suffering!

Job's friends did not understand this. They couldn't conceptualize this because oftentimes, *'religious'* people who don't have (or maintain) an active relationship with (*or a connection to*) God will judge another person's life and their circumstances based on the surface-level *knowledge* that they have about God. These judgments are not based on actually experiencing God for themselves. Therefore, these types of surface-level, appearance-based judgments are often arrogant, erroneous, and inaccurate.

What Job was going through was an experience with God. An experience with God is much deeper than knowledge of God. Without experiencing God, you cannot have a true relationship/connection with Him. In fact, I'm convinced that you cannot truly know God without experiencing Him for yourself.

Knowledge of an apple is much different than tasting it for yourself. You can study an apple for decades and explain all kinds of facts about the apple, but until you taste one for yourself, your knowledge is only surface-level. Until you experience the sweetness, the crunch, and the juice of an apple, then you can only describe details that you learned about the apple. Those details will be shallow, meaningless, and lacking the depth of experience and encounter.

When you're going through despair, some of the best help you can get is people who can empathize and have also experienced what you're experiencing. Knowledge is more surface-level, so those people who try to offer you knowledge-based comfort in your time of grief and despair can only offer you surface-level advice that does NOT reach into the depths of your despair. This is a grossly improper way to comfort someone. It is especially terrible if that surface-level advice turns into surface-level accusations, as in the case of Job and his *friends*. Job exclaims:

"I have heard all this before.
What miserable comforters you are!" —Job 16:2 NLT

Sometimes, just being present and being quiet is the best thing you can do to comfort someone who is going through grief or despair. Sitting WITH THEM in their despair can be powerful. There is great power in "presence." To know that you are not alone in your deepest, darkest moments is comfort all by itself. Presence is power!

The Bible says:

"Rejoice with those who rejoice, and weep with those who weep."
—Romans 12:15 NKJV

Job actually voices this wise advice on comforting to his friends when he says to them:

"If only you could be silent!
That's the wisest thing you can do."
—Job 13:5 NLT

"I will defend my own ways before Him."
—Job 13:15 NKJV

At last, we have come back to our subject verse for this chapter. The second half of Job 13:15! Now, we see the full context of what Job is saying, when he says *"Though He slay me, yet will I trust Him. Even so, I will defend my own ways before Him."* *—Job 13:15 NKJV*

Job is making a defense for his innocence against his friends who keep suggesting that the bad things that had happened to Job were because of his sin. Job is actually attempting to "speak to the Almighty" himself and plead his [Job's] case (*Job 13:3*). The pain and weight of suffering mixed with the bombardment of accusations of sin from his friends has pushed Job to the point that he is fed up and wants to plead his case with the Lord God Himself. This idea frightens Job because Job still fears *(honors and respects)* the Lord. *"Though He slay me, yet will I trust Him."* Job has experienced darkness after darkness, and he has had enough!

My Darkness

October 24th, 2022. This is the date when one of my worst fears came true. This is the date when I experienced what Job mentioned in Chapter 3 verse 25, *"What I always feared has happened to me. What I dreaded has come true."* What I dreaded most had happened to me. I received a call at work just after lunch.

My mother died unexpectedly. Waves of thoughts and emotions washed over me and consumed me. Shock, disbelief, confusion, disorientation, deep pain, deep hurt, and deep sorrow. I felt utterly crushed. Crushed to the point of numbness. Crushed to the point of despair. Dread led to distress. Distress led to despair. Despair led to darkness. And darkness had overtaken me. Sheer and utter darkness. I felt hopeless and without a sense of direction on how to get myself out.

And to be honest, I didn't have a desire to get out of that darkness. The hurt was so deep that it totally shattered my will to exist. I was numb to all feelings except pain. I could have lain down in a fetal position and cried myself to sleep, and then slept a deep sleep. Sleep until I didn't wake up.

Unlike Job in his troubles, I DO have a loving, supportive wife and family and friends who love me deeply and who tried to comfort me. However, the pain was so hurtful, and the darkness was so deep that I was too far beyond their reach. I had fallen so deep into the dark, nothingness that I was beyond anyone's ability or capability to reach me. I appreciated their love and attempts at comfort, but this was a darkness that no human being could get me out of. It was a darkness that I couldn't get myself out of. A darkness that I had no desire to get out of.

My Light! Who's There?!

This was the darkest place I had ever been in spiritually, mentally, and emotionally. Despair and hopelessness were the constant atmosphere in that cold, dark place. The hopelessness was suffocating me, and I didn't care. I just wanted to sit in despair and go numb and still and lifeless. But, in that darkness, in that pit, I realized something peculiar. I was not alone! There was a presence there with me! I felt a familiar presence, and it was warm.

Have you ever felt that someone was behind you or in a room with you when you thought you were alone, so you turned your head quickly in that direction to see "who's there"?! That's what this felt like. A very real presence. And this was a warm presence, unlike the cold despair that I was in. I've felt this presence before! It was Jesus!! My Savior! My REAL-LIFE SAVIOR! My light!

Power in Presence

Jesus was there WITH ME in the darkness. With me IN my despair! Even as I type this, tears are pouring from my face into my T-shirt and onto my dining room table, not out of pain but from a place of profound thankfulness. Even thinking back on it, I am overwhelmed with gratefulness to the Lord for the fact that He was present. Present WITH ME! Letting me know that I was not alone. I was no longer hopeless. He was WITH ME! He was with me when no one else COULD reach me.

I'm not telling you about a 'Jesus' that I read about or studied, or someone told me about. I'm talking about at my lowest, most hurtful moment in life, I experiencing the presence of a VERY REAL Jesus at my lowest, most hurtful moment in life. And, it wasn't anything specific that He said to me. It was just the simple fact that He was there! His presence alone provided hope in my hopelessness, warmth in my cold despair, and light in my darkness. The eternal King of Kings and Lord of Lords got off of His throne, crawled down into my pit of despair, and loved me back to life again! Then, He reassured me that with HIS help and strength, this was a pain that I could live with. He reassured me that He would ALWAYS be with me. ALWAYS and in ALL WAYS! Even in the pit of darkness and despair, He IS with me!

"If I ascend into heaven, You are there;
If I make my bed in hell, behold, You are there."
—Psalms 139:8 NKJV

Love Me Back to Life

When Jesus snatched me back to life from my darkness, I became aware of my surroundings, and my wife's arms were wrapped around me in an embrace of warm love. I didn't spend too much time in despair; however, anyone who has been in dark hopelessness can tell you that ANY time you spend in darkness feels like a long time.

Writing this, I'm reminded of the old hymn lyrics "Love Lifted Me," which goes:

"Love lifted me!
Love lifted me!
When nothing else could help
Love lifted me!
Souls in danger, look above, Jesus completely saves
He will lift you by His love, out of the angry waves
He's the Master of the sea, billows His will obey
He your Savior wants to be, be saved today…"

With my wife's arms wrapped around me, I wept silently as I became so overwhelmed with love because I realized what had just happened to me. Jesus had loved me back to LIFE! The Resurrected King used His presence and His love to resurrect me from darkness to light. Back from no desire to continue living to "there IS hope!" He loved me back to a place where I was able to receive the love of my wife and family/friends. For this, I am ever grateful to MY Lord Jesus Christ! The lover of my soul!

Light Shines in Darkness

I don't know what darkness you have gone (*or are going*) through. Truthfully, no one fully knows. My darkness doesn't look like your darkness. My pain doesn't look like your pain. My suffering doesn't look like Job's suffering or your suffering. My place of despair and hopelessness is not quite the same as yours. We all have our own darknesses. No one can fully understand your darkness except someone who was/is there WITH you. My brother, my sister, PLEASE understand this truth: ONLY Jesus can fully understand your darkness because ONLY He can be (was) there WITH YOU in the darkness. And just like He was the light in my darkness, He can and will be the light in yours!

Suffering Brings Proximity, Proximity Brings Revelation

Our suffering, painful as it may be, provides a unique opportunity for us that only suffering can provide. Suffering brings God closer to us to see things about Him that we would not have seen otherwise.

As the Bible states in *Psalms 34:18 NLT, "The Lord is close to the brokenhearted; He rescues those whose spirits are crushed."*

God is near to the broken-hearted. And when you are near someone, you are able to see details about them that you couldn't see from further away. And when you are in closer proximity to the Eternal God, you are able to see eternal details (aka *"revelations"*).

When God is nearer to us in our suffering, we are in a position to gain priceless revelation about Him. Think of a father hugging his child after the child has fallen and hurt themselves. The Father comes closer (*nearer*) to comfort the child in an embrace. However, while the father is close, the child is able to notice details about their father that they may not have known before. Maybe the child notices the smell of the father's soap, deodorant, or aftershave. Or the curl pattern of the father's beard. Or the amount of gray hair that the father has (*of which this writer has many* ☺). Or maybe the child notices the rhythm of their father's heartbeat. These are all details that most people cannot tell you about the man because they have never shared that type of nearness as the man's child has.

Our suffering brings us into closer proximity with God, which allows us to see details about our eternal Father that other people don't get to see outside of suffering. These *"eternal details"* are called *"revelation."* God is revealed to us in our suffering!

Jesus is the Hidden Jewel

By the time we reach Job in chapter 13 verse 15, he has gone through unimaginable suffering. Adding to his pain and grief, Job has received discouragement from his wife and multiple insults and accusations from his *friends*. There is no comfort or relief to be found in ANY of the people closest to Job. Remember, *"When you're going through despair, some of the best help you can get is people who can empathize and have also experienced what you've experienced."*

Job is exhausted, hurting, and fed up with the false accusations of his sin. So, he wants to plead his case with God himself, but he STILL honors God so much that he [Job] understands that he can't just stand before God (*who is the righteous Judge of all the Earth*) and plead innocence (Job 9:1-4). So, Job longs for help, a *'mediator'* who can plead his case to God (Job 9:32-35).

Now, Job's suffering and lack of comfort put him in a position where he longs for something that he does not currently have, but so desperately needs. A mediator between himself and God, and a proper comforter. Someone who can stand in the presence of God and make intercession on Job's behalf. Job was longing for Jesus!! Job's distress and despair, his need for comfort, his defense of innocence, and his request for a mediator all point in the same direction. Jesus! Job wants *"...a way that I could speak to Him [God] and plead my case"* (Job 13:3). Jesus is "the Way" that Job is longing for (John 14:6), and He [Jesus] mediates for us.

Job's suffering has led him to cry out for Jesus Christ, his Savior! Now, Job did not call "Jesus" by name since he [Job] was alive thousands of years before Jesus walked the Earth. Job did, however, describe Jesus in his cry out for a "mediator" and "intercessor" between God and mankind. This is exactly what Jesus is to and for us! He intercedes and mediates FOR US with God.

Look at what the Bible says in Romans 8:33-39 (NIV).

"Who will bring any charge against those whom God has chosen? It is God who justifies.
Who then is the one who condemns? No one. Christ Jesus who died—more than that, who was raised to life—is at the right hand of God and is also interceding for us.
Who shall separate us from the love of Christ? Shall trouble or hardship or persecution or famine or nakedness or danger or sword?
As it is written: "For your sake we face death all day long; we are considered as sheep to be slaughtered."
No, in all these things we are more than conquerors through him who loved us.
For I am convinced that neither death nor life, neither angels nor demons, neither the present nor the future, nor any powers,
neither height nor depth, nor anything else in all creation, will be able to separate us from the love of God that is in Christ Jesus our Lord."

I purposely included verses *35 through 39* because I believe they apply so well to Job's story and also to remind us that when we are going through our own suffering, Jesus is constantly with us and will never leave us!

Jesus has experienced more suffering than ANYONE EVER, so He is best qualified and able to identify WITH US and to comfort us in our suffering. He is the best person to be WITH US in our darkness.

Search for the Light

Job was filled, surrounded, and overcome with darkness. And this darkness prodded *(goad-poked)* Job *(see the last chapter)* to search for light (*hope*). The light that Job was looking for is The Light (The Hope) of the world, Jesus Christ!

In your deepest darkness, you need light. You need Eternal Light to give you hope, comfort, and warmth in your cold, dark despair. That light gives you an assurance that you are not alone. You, like Job, need Jesus! Jesus is the light (and hope) of the world!

> *"The light [Jesus] shines in the darkness, and the darkness CAN NEVER extinguish it." —John 1:5 NLT*

Let me translate that verse for you so you can use it as a reminder of hope in your dark seasons and dark moments in life.

Jesus is WITH YOU in your darkness, and He brings light, warmth, hope, peace, and comfort that your darkness CAN NEVER extinguish!

In your darkness, declare what God declared from the very beginning: "Let there be light!" Let there be hope! Let there be peace! Let there be warmth and comfort in your despair! Let there be Jesus WITH YOU, loving you back to life again!

Lean in and pay close attention because this is where we go tremendously deep (to the core) to uncover how profound this hidden treasure in Job's story truly is!

The 'Crown Jewel' of Job

Throughout this chapter, I mention that there is more value hidden within the context of the text in Job 13:15. Let me show you just how valuable that hidden treasure is!

This is what I call 'The Crown Jewel' of Job's story! The most precious, most valuable piece of the whole story. In a story FULL of beautiful, timeless gems of wisdom and insight, this part is thee most valuable. And no, it's not the end of Job's story when God blesses Job twice over for everything that he lost (Job 42:10-13). Nor is it the fact that God allowed Job to live 140 years after his trials to be able to see four generations of his children and grandchildren (Job 42:16-17). The crown jewel of Job is found right in the middle of Job's suffering in chapter 19, verse 25.

> *"For I know that my Redeemer lives, A*
> *nd He shall stand at last on the earth."*
> *—Job 19:25 NKJV*

Take a few seconds to **REALLY** let the power and impact of that statement sink into your heart and mind.

For you to understand the **FULL power** of that statement, you first have to understand a few details about Job. Job is considered, by many scholars and theologians, as one of the oldest (*if not thee oldest*) written books in the Bible. Job existed long before Moses (*who wrote the first five books of the Bible*) and long before King David (*whom the promised Messiah, Savior would eventually be born into).* Job also existed long before any Israelite prophecy of a Savior (*Redeemer*) coming to earth to save us all. In fact, Job is not an Israelite at all! The Bible doesn't tell us that Job was circumcised and in a covenant relationship with God. Job existed long before Jacob (Israel), Isaac, and maybe even Abraham.

I personally believe that Job existed in a time that was after Noah and before Abraham (Abram) because of what God says about Job in chapter 1, verse 8 (NKJV).

"Then the Lord said to Satan, 'Have you considered My servant Job, that there is NONE like him on earth, a blameless and upright man, one who fears God and shuns evil?'"

If God is bragging that there is **NO ONE on earth** that is like this man, then I believe God in that there is no one like Job on earth at the time.

I tell you these details to get you to understand the context in which Job makes his statement in chapter 19, verse 25. Job has no Bible, Scripture, or commandments from God to reference, no promise from God to look forward to, and no prophets to give him hope for the future. All Job has is a connection with God and an experience with God through suffering. In this suffering, Job is allowed access to be in closer proximity to God, which leads him to revelation. Job experienced some of the worst suffering any human being could ever imagine, and as a result, Job received one of the deepest revelations about God EVER!! An invaluable, eternal treasure! And Job had access to this eternal treasure BEFORE Abraham, Isaac, Jacob, Joseph, Moses, David, and all the prophets! Before them all, Job prophesies out of his pain and says: "I KNOW that my Redeemer [Jesus] LIVES *And He SHALL stand at last on the earth."*

This means that Job knew Jesus (his Redeemer) was alive RIGHT NOW, but not yet on earth. Job also knew that one day, his Redeemer (Jesus) would stand on the earth *(was coming).*

How?! How is it possible that you are alive but not on earth? Only God can accomplish this! Only God can be 'alive,' not on earth, but will come to the earth at a future time to redeem us.

Job received revelation of God's plan to redeem the world thousands of years before Jesus was ever born and long before any prophet ever prophesied about the Messiah (Savior).

This shows us how truly powerful an experience with God is and how great of an opportunity our suffering can be for us. They can lead us to God, showing us things that He has not shown ANYONE else! Suffering can lead us to God, revealing to us His very being!

Jesus is the crowned jewel that was hidden in the dark context of Job's story of suffering! Jesus is the hidden crowned jewel in the context of your darkness and your suffering. Don't miss Him! Look for the Light. Your light!

Questions for You to Ponder

Can you trust God even though it SEEMS like He is *'slaying'* you? Can you trust God when you don't understand Him? Can you trust Him to understand that He has an overall plan for your good, even though He may have allowed some evil to happen to you? Can you trust that His plan is eternal and much larger than you?

Thousands and thousands of years later, we are still gleaning from Job's suffering. Can God use you in this way? To help other generations to trust Him and to have a relationship and connection with Him?

Will you allow Jesus to be the light in your darkness? Will you allow Him to comfort you like no one else can? Your friends and family may love you dearly, but they cannot be WITH you and comfort you through EVERY situation. Only God can do that through Jesus Christ and by the power of His Holy Spirit! Let Jesus comfort you, warm you, lead you, and reveal His Truth to you with His light! Let Jesus call you out of darkness into His marvelous light! (1 Peter 2:9)

Prayer: Lord, when my soul is crushed, and it feels like I'm being destroyed by darkness. I sometimes feel that I'm in a place of total despair beyond the reach of anyone. But I know that you are with me! You have promised to NEVER leave me, nor will you forsake me (Hebrews 13:5). You have promised to be with me even to the end of time (Matthew 28:20). Even if I made my bed in the lowest, darkest, most hopeless place, you are with me (Psalms 139:8). So, even though it seems that I am surrounded and filled with total darkness and despair, in my desperation, I KNOW that you are HERE WITH ME! I KNOW that my Redeemer LIVES!! I know that you have ALREADY won the victory for me. I take comfort in the mere fact that you are present WITH ME. I understand that you may not snatch me out of this pit immediately, and my circumstances may not change immediately. I'm okay with that because I know that YOU WILL NEVER LEAVE ME!

Comfort me like only you can by the power of your Holy Spirit. Help me to have patient endurance through my suffering because I know it won't last always (1 Peter 5:10). And help me to lean on your strength in my weakness (2 Corinthians 12:9-

10). When I am weak, you are strong. Thank you for your presence in my despair. Thank you for your comfort in my hurt. Thank you for your strength in my weakness. Thank you for your light that shines in my darkness and never fails. Thank you for allowing me to suffer because I now know it will not only bear good fruit in my life but also someone else's life, and it will give you eternal Glory! In Jesus' name, Amen!!

A little something you may have overlooked: The Bible didn't say that Satan healed the wounds that HE caused Job or replenished Job's wealth or blessed Job with children after causing his [Job's] initial children to die. This is because Satan CANNOT restore or heal. He ONLY takes and destroys. The Bible DOES say that GOD restores Job (Job 42:10-17). This is because every good and perfect gift comes from the Lord (James 1:17). The thief [Satan] comes ONLY to steal, to kill, and to destroy, but I [Jesus] have come that they might have life and life more abundantly (John 10:10).

CHAPTER 4
God Don't Like Ugly

By: Minister John Davidson Jr.

Church folk love this phrase! They quote it like it's an absolute truth. And to be honest, it sounds as if it could be true. Because God created a beautiful world, so He can't like 'ugly', right? Ugly is bad, and God is good, and God doesn't like 'bad'! Does He?!

We know from the previous two chapters that this statement is not entirely correct. However, unlike the previous two chapters, this phrase *"God don't (doesn't) like ugly"* is not Scripture at all, nor does it have any scriptural reference.

What the Bible actually says about God and appearances is found in 1 Samuel 16:7 (NLT):

> "But the Lord said to Samuel, 'Don't judge by his ***appearance*** or height, for I have rejected him. ***The Lord doesn't see things the way you see them.*** People judge by the ***outward appearance,*** but ***the Lord looks at the heart.***"

This verse is in the context of God using the prophet Samuel to select and anoint the next king of Israel. Samuel looks at one of Jesse's sons, Eliab, who is tall, and thinks to himself that, based on his height, he is the obvious choice. But God tells Samuel that He [God] does not look at appearances, but instead looks at hearts. Not height, but heart. In other words, human beings judge based on surface-level appearances, but God looks deeper, beyond the surface into the core (*heart*).

As it relates to the phrase *"God don't like ugly,"* people normally use it when relating to *ugly* words, actions, and behaviors of another person. Growing up, I would typically hear this phrase from people using it as an explanation for what they perceived as a 'consequence'. For instance, if a little boy calls another little boy a mean name, and then immediately afterward, he [the first little boy] trips over a toy. The response from a teacher or someone older would be, *"See there?! God don't like ugly*!" Or if a little girl doesn't share her toys with other little girls, and then her toy breaks. *"See there?! God don't like ugly!"* It's used in a way (*and as a way*) to discourage negative behavior by attributing consequences to those negative behaviors, even if those *'consequences'* were mere coincidences. It's used as if it is an explanation of God's judgment and justice.

Now, I want to be very clear. God IS a God of justice; as the Bible states in Psalms 89:14 and Jerimiah 9:24.

*"**Righteousness and justice are the foundation of your [God's] throne**. Unfailing love and truth walk before you as attendants."*
—Psalms 89:14 NLT

*"But those who wish to boast should boast in this alone: that they **truly know me and understand that I am the Lord** who demonstrates unfailing love and who **brings justice** and **righteousness** to the earth, and that I delight in these things. I, the Lord have spoken!"*
—Jeremiah 9:24 NLT

You Reap What You Sow

In Galatians chapter 6 verse 7 (NKJV), the Apostle Paul says,

> *"Do not be deceived, God is not mocked; for whatever a man sows, that he will also reap."*

This speaks to the justice of God as being a law of nature that God has established on earth for all of time.

If you plant an orange seed, then you'll grow an orange tree that bears orange fruit. You CANNOT plant an orange seed and grow bananas or grapes. Orange seeds ONLY produce oranges. If you sow deceit, deception, discord and division, then you should expect to reap the results of that deceit, deception, discord and division as the fruit of your labor. You're getting paid for the work you've done.

Justice and Mercy

Sowing and reaping is a law of nature that God has established, and it cannot, does not, and will not change. It remains as consistent as God's nature. God is a just and righteous God.

Even God coming to the Earth in the form of Jesus Christ to die for our sins is a display of God's justice. In fact, Jesus dying on the cross is the perfect display of God's justice and mercy working together simultaneously.

The wages of sin (*death*) that we all earn ***(Romans 6:23)*** but can't afford to pay ***(Colossians 2:13-14)*** was *covered* on the cross by Jesus' life and shed blood. Amen! This is God's ultimate justice as payment for all sin. But it is also God's mercy ("*...the* *free gift of God" —Romans 6:23*) by sparing us the cost of paying for **our own** sins.

In other words, God shows us His justice and mercy because He satisfied the cost of OUR sin with HIS death through Jesus Christ. This is good news! In fact, it's The Good News, the Gospel that we now have an opportunity to have a **relationship** with God through Jesus Christ and what He did on the cross, **even though** we have all earned death due to our sins. Now, we can have a relationship with and a connection to God. ***(Ephesians 2:1-18)***

Cost of Death vs Cost of Consequences

Even though God spared us the cost of death, it does not mean that we don't have to pay the cost of consequences. Jesus died to spare us from the wages of sin, which is death. So, we no longer have to die for our sins, but this **does not** mean that we get to avoid the consequences of the choices that we make. The principal truth of sewing and reaping still exists.

Let's say you become a Believer in Jesus Christ and then go back to your old, sinful ways and steal a car. Your soul is saved from eternal damnation, but you will still go to jail for your crime. God will not be mocked; whatever you sow, that you will also reap. Cause and effect.

"If you confess with your mouth that Jesus is Lord and believe in your heart that God raised him from the dead, you will be saved. For it is by believing in your heart that you are made right with God, and it is by confessing with your mouth that you are saved." —Romans 10:9-10 NLT

These verses reveal to us how our souls are saved, but that doesn't mean that we can do whatever we want and keep on sinning without consequence.

"Well then, should we keep on sinning so that God can show us more and more of his wonderful grace? Of course not! Since we have died to sin, how can we continue to live in it?"
—Romans 6:1-2 NLT

"Dear friends, if we deliberately continue sinning after we have received knowledge of the truth, there is no longer any sacrifice that will cover these sins. There is only the terrible expectation of God's judgment and the raging fire that will consume his enemies."
—Hebrews 10:26-27 NLT

Sometimes, consequences serve as a form of God's discipline, keeping us off of dangerous paths in life. This is an act of love because it ultimately benefits our overall well-being. *(Good FOR us, but not good TO us.)*

"For the LORD disciplines those he loves,
and he punishes each one He accepts as his child."
—Hebrews 12:6 NLT

Judgment & Justice

So, what does this have to do with "God don't like ugly"? It helps us understand that God is a God of justice, and this phrase was/is used to speak to God's justice. However, the phrase is misleading because God's judgment and justice doesn't look like ours. God doesn't judge using the same criteria that we do (*surface-level appearances*). Also, God's justice comes WITH grace, mercy, and unfailing love. So much unfailing love that God Himself [Jesus] was willing to die for us to save us from the death sentence that we all earn from our sins. God's judgment and justice look nothing like what we call *judgment* and *justice.*

Therefore, using the phrase "God don't like ugly" when a person is receiving what **APPEARS** on the surface to be a consequence of an action does not apply to the situation because it does not correctly represent God in the matter. We can't see the heart of a person or situation, nor do we have the eternal perspective to judge something as *good* or *bad*. Therefore, we could potentially be erroneous in calling something God's judgment/justice when it may not necessarily be so, much like Job's friends (*see the last chapter*).

So, yes, God is a God of justice, implementing sowing and reaping. But that does not necessarily mean that God does not like *ugly*.

Does God Like Ugly?

When we use the phrase "God don't like ugly," we misunderstand and misrepresent the sovereignty of God the Almighty. We're talking about a perfect God who does not need or require perfection from His creation to produce something good and beautiful. This is illustrated in how God creates the world and then reviews His creation to see that it is "good," not "perfect."

We must understand that God is the Creator and the source of creativity, which means He's the most creative One of all. And as the most creative One, God doesn't need the best materials to create something "good" and beautiful.

As I mentioned two chapters ago:

"It's easy to create something 'good' when you're using all the best materials. That doesn't make you creative; it makes you an assembler. You've simply assembled materials that were already "good." The ***true test*** *of creativity is in what you can create using less-than-desirable materials.*

God displays His creative mastery by using good AND bad things to create good, beautiful things. To take it a step further, ***God shows the vastness of His creativity by creating good FROM bad. Bringing out beauty from the ugly.****"*

God is not afraid of what we call *ugly*. He uses *ugly,* like an artist painting a masterpiece using a color that people may consider undesirable.

Think of the color black. Now, imagine a scenario where many people feel the color black is hideous, harsh, and heinous. However, a truly creative artist looks at the color black as beautiful and necessary for his/her masterpiece! The artist sees all the potential uses that black has and the infinite possibilities that can be created using the color. Mixing black with other colors to create darker tones adds depth and density to an artwork. Laying jet black against a lighter color enhances and highlights the color, setting it apart from the rest of the painting and adding depth to an underwater piece, or a sky black to present the beauty in a night sky decorated with stars and constellations. The artist looks beyond the appearance that others see and sees the potential and value.

God is more than a creative artist. He is thee Creator. He looks beyond the appearance of a person, situation, or relationship and sees what it is at its core. This allows God to see true value and potential.

Therefore, what we consider 'ugly,' God considers 'raw material.' In the same way that a lump of clay is ugly to some people, but to the potter, the lump is beautiful because of its potential. We see the ugly in our lives and want to judge it or discard it. God considers that same ugly for its potential to be beautiful.

Missed Value

God is not afraid of ugly because He sees the true value that is beyond the surface appearance, just like an antique found in someone's home. It would be a tragic waste to discard the antique without having it appraised to understand its true value.

Because of God's oversight, insight, and foresight, He is best able to assess the actual value of a thing. And as One who sees and understands, God is best able to redeem a thing, person, or situation based on that true value.

Christ the Redeemer!

We don't always see the value in ugly. God, the Creator, IS creativity. Which means that He finds value where others don't. And He redeems that value because He knows the true value of something regardless of its appearance. While some people may consider *ugly* as something to throw away, Jesus sees ugly as something to redeem.

Jesus Christ IS our Redeemer. Christ the Redeemer!

> [20]*"The Redeemer will come to Zion, And to those who turn from transgression in Jacob," Says the LORD.*
> *—Isaiah 59:20 NKJV*

> *[19]"For God in all His fullness was pleased to live in Christ,*
> *[20]and through Him God reconciled everything to Himself. He made peace with everything in heaven and on earth by means of Christ's blood on the cross.*
> *[21]This includes you who were once far away from God. You were His enemies, separated from Him by your evil thoughts and actions.*
> *[22]Yet now He has reconciled you to Himself through the death of Christ in His physical body. As a result, He has brought you into his own presence, and you are holy and blameless as you stand before Him without a single fault."*
> *—Colossians 1:19-22 NKJV*

> *"Christ has redeemed us from the curse of the law, having become a curse for us (for it is written, 'Cursed is everyone who hangs on a tree')." —Galatians 3:13 NKJV*

To redeem means to buy back, recover, or pay off. Jesus repurchased us (*reclaimed* us) from sin by paying the wages of sin, which is death. In other words, sin says that we are worth nothing and should be thrown away (*death*). Throw the *ugly* away! Conversely, Jesus refuses to throw us away because He believes that we are worth much more. Much, much more!

What are we worth? What is our true value to God?

By paying the ultimate price (His LIFE), Jesus shows us how much we are **worth**. We are worth **the very life of the King of Kings and Lord of Lords**! The Creator of all thinks that we are invaluable. Priceless! So much so that He sacrificed His very life for us! And this wasn't just ANY life. This was the life of eternal royalty!

> *"I [Jesus] and My Father are one." —John 10:30 NKJV*

Jesus IS God! So, when He [Jesus] sacrificed Himself, He was sacrificing the life of God! That is an extremely high price to pay for us, worthless sinners! That while we were yet sinners, Christ died for us ***(Romans 5:6-11).*** This is an unfathomable, unspeakable amount of love.

> [16]*"For God so loved the world that He gave His only begotten Son, that whoever believes in Him should not perish but have everlasting life.*
> [17]*"For God did not send His Son into the world to condemn the world, but that the world through Him might be saved."*
> *— John 3:16-17 NKJV*

I have *never* heard of *any* earthly king who sacrificed his own life for his citizens. Jesus bought us with His very own life to show us what we are truly worth. The value of a thing is measured and indicated by how much it costs.

The life of the King of Kings and Lord of Lords is what we are worth! And since we are so valuable, we should not sell ourselves short and live a life that is beneath this value. Instead, we should try to live up to this value.

What Was Job *Really* Saying?!

Let's revisit a powerful verse that I mentioned in the last chapter, which I call the "Crown Jewel of Job".

> *"For I know that my Redeemer lives, And He shall stand at last on the earth;" —Job 19:25 NKJV*

We can now truly appreciate the core (*not the surface*) of what Job is saying in this verse. We see here that Job's remarkable statement is not just a statement of incredible faith and hope but also one of beautiful transformation. What Job is saying is that with all of this *ugly* that he was experiencing at that moment in his life, he **knows** that he has someone who will **redeem** the ugly and **turn it** into beauty. Job knew that his Redeemer would take all that ugly and creatively transform, repurpose, and revalue it into something beautiful!

Real-life Redeemer

It's been my experience that God works well with imperfect things; turning them into masterpieces. This is not just true in Job's life, but I have seen it up close.

My mother was the fourth-oldest child of nine children. Due to the lifestyle that my grandmother chose to live at the time, my mother had the responsibility of practically raising her five younger siblings as a sort of 'momma-sister.' She was often left to care for her younger siblings. This responsibility deprived my mother of a full childhood as she was forced to grow up fast. To exponentially multiply the hardship and suffering of a little girl, my mother was also inappropriately abused by an uncle. She endured things that no human being, much less a little girl, should ever have to suffer or endure.

Robbed of her childhood and stripped of her innocence, my mother showed incomparable strength and tenacity by maintaining excellent grades in school up until she graduated high school (*with honors*). She carried this excellence into her college years and graduated from a business school (*with honors*) to receive her associate's degree in accounting. My mother believed in the *American Dream,* which holds that if you get good grades and work really hard, then you can secure a job that pays well and can change your life for the better. Unfortunately, this was not altogether true for a poor black girl from the East Side (*ghetto*) of Buffalo, NY, regardless of how brilliant of a mind she had.

This was a huge disappointment to my mother. It destroyed her hope. Proverbs 13:12 (NLT) states that *"Hope deferred makes the heart sick, but a dream fulfilled is a tree of life."*

With her hopes deferred, heart sickened, and dreams unfulfilled, my mother shifted her hopes and dreams and placed them elsewhere. She placed her hopes into something that promised quicker results. The streets! Unfortunately, my mother turned to quick money. Much of this *quick money* came from *'street pharmaceuticals'* also known as *drug dealing*.

The late 1970s to the early 1980s was unfortunately a very opportune time to enter the illegal drug game. Just towards the end of the heroine era and right at the start of the crack era, you could say that this was a *"sweet spot"* to begin a career selling illegal drugs. Demand was extremely high, as was supply; and you were all but guaranteed repeat *customers*.

This was an era where a smart black girl could take her brilliant mind for learning and creatively mix it with some *street knowledge* to make quick money selling little rocks to get people high.

Mixing science and arithmetic. Mixing measurements and mathematics. Chemistry with accounting. Replacing school labs with kitchen labs; and lab scales and lab tools with kitchen scales and kitchen utensils.

Ingenuity and creativity *seemed* to provide a way for deferred dreams to be realized; at least partially. This was an opportunity for a better life, though the means were *ugly*.

My mother experienced some success in the streets, but it also came with extreme risk and some tough losses as well. Much like the users of the drugs, the sellers experience very high highs and extremely low lows.

It was a rollercoaster that was headed for destruction until she hit a big 'halt' in 1985. She got pregnant with my sister, and then one year later, she gave birth to me.

Being the loving nurturer that she was, my mother refused to raise her children in the destructive lifestyle that she was living. She also did not want to raise us around any of the dark influences, cycles, and trauma she experienced. So, she decided to place her hope elsewhere. But this time she put her hope in a Redeemer who can take old, ugly things and make them new! She turned to Jesus, and He TOTALLY turned her life around.

She took some training, got certified, and then began to work at the VA hospital as a pharmacist tech. There, she met my stepfather. They moved us 1,200 miles away from Buffalo, NY, to New Orleans, LA. They married, had another child (*my brother*), and raised my sister, myself, and my brother there in the church, where I heard plenty of old church sayings that I am currently writing about today!

We were raised knowing the Lord Jesus Christ **for ourselves** and encouraged to develop a personal relationship with Him! We NEVER had to experience the trauma and abuse that my mother experienced as a child because of the changes that she allowed God to make in her life.

My mother was NOT a broken, traumatized little girl whose life should be thrown away in the streets. Glory to God! He looked beyond the surface and saw her true value, that she was priceless and worth dying for. She was worth the life of the Eternal King! So, He paid for her, redeemed and revalued her!

God healed trauma and transformed it into triumph! He took an ugly childhood and redeemed it into a beautiful childhood for my siblings and I. Jesus took my mother from selling illegal drugs on the street, *hurting people in the process,* and redeemed that ugly into a beautiful, **30-year career as a pharmacist tech**, issuing LEGAL drugs to veterans, helping them with their ailments and traumas!

I share this story with you to display to you the real-life redemptive power of Jesus Christ in hopes that you will invite Him into the *ugly* in your life and let Him rework it into something beautiful.

Ugly Jesus! Ugly Cross!

The most proof that we have of God not having the same apprehension to what we call '*ugly*' is Jesus Himself. Was Jesus ugly? No! I'm not saying that at all. However, Jesus' appearance was not what many of us may imagine it to be. Listen to how Isaiah describes Jesus in a prophesy approximately 700 years before Jesus is born.

> *"1 My servant [Jesus] grew up in the LORD's presence like a tender green shoot, like a root in dry ground.*
> *2 There was nothing beautiful or majestic about his appearance, nothing to attract us to Him.*
> *3 He was despised and rejected—a man of sorrows, acquainted with deepest grief. (See how Jesus relates to Job.)*
> *We turned our backs on Him [Jesus] and looked the other way. He was despised, and we did not care.*

> [4]*Yet it was OUR weaknesses He carried; it was OUR sorrows that weighed Him down. And we thought His troubles were a punishment from God. (Like Job's friends thought of his troubles as a punishment.)*
> [5]*But He was pierced for OUR rebellion, crushed for OUR sins. He was beaten so we could be whole. He was whipped so we could be healed."*
> *—Isaiah 53:2-5 NLT (Emphasis added)*

Notice how Isaiah says that nothing was beautiful or majestic or attractive about Jesus' appearance. The King of Kings did not choose the most beautiful body to be born into. Isaiah also gives us a picture of what God's justice looks like. It is not what it appears to be on the surface. God takes our *ugly* onto Himself to pay the debt that WE owe. This is true justice AND mercy at the same time because it satisfies the cost WHILE freeing the guilty (us).

So, we see here that Isaiah 53:2-5 stands firmly against the phrase "God don't like ugly" because it affirms Gods justice regardless of how *'ugly'* the appearance.

The appearance of Jesus' death was also quite ugly indeed! His clothes were torn off and was tortured before dying an extremely gruesome death.

He was whipped with a whip that had metal pieces or sharp bone pieces at the tips. The whip would deliver a lightening strike of pain throughout Jesus' body and mind simultaneously upon immediate contact just before ripping away flesh once yanked away. Jesus' back muscles and joints would have been exposed and running with blood. Thorns from a hand-crafted *"crown"* made from a thorn bush was pressed into His skull all around Jesus' head which caused blood poured down His face and neck. He was slapped, punched, spat upon, cursed at, and beaten unrecognizable.

> *"But many were amazed when they saw Him [Jesus]. His face was so disfigured He seemed hardly human, and from His appearance, one would scarcely know He was a man."*
> *—Isaiah 52:14 NLT*

To crescendo the pain and torture, 7–9-inch nails were driven through Jesus' wrist and feet to nail Him to an approximately 300-hundred-pound, wooden cross. There He hung with His arms stretched wide, naked, bloody, beaten, and in remarkable, unimaginable pain. And innocent. There He hung for roughly 6 hours until giving up His last breath. Could you imagine being slowly choked for 6 hours?! Could you imagine the colossal amount of pain that Jesus experienced? Can you fathom the frequency of pain that was shrieking through His body and mind?!

Jesus' death was gruesome. Extremely ugly! Yet, He did not despise the ugliness of the death on the cross.

> *"...And let us run with endurance the race God has set before us. We do this by keeping our eyes on Jesus, the champion who initiates and perfects our faith. Because of the joy awaiting Him, He endured the cross, disregarding its shame. Now He is seated in the place of honor beside God's throne."*
> *—Hebrews 12:2 NLT*

In other words, Jesus was despised (Isaiah 53:3), but did not despise the cross (Hebrews 12:2). He was hated, but He did not hate the ugly things that He would have to suffer. Instead, He looked past the ugly and saw the beauty of salvation that would come from the ugliness of the cross. This gave (and gives) Jesus joy! And it pleases God The Father as well.

> *But it was the LORD's good plan to crush Him [Jesus] and cause Him grief. Yet when His life is made an offering for sin, He will have many descendants. He will enjoy a long life, and the LORD's good plan will prosper in His [Jesus'] hands. When He [Jesus] sees all that is accomplished by His anguish, He will be satisfied. And because of His experience, my righteous servant will make it possible for many to be counted righteous for He will bear all their sins."*
> *—Isaiah 53:10-11 NLT*

It was God's GOOD plan that His Son, Jesus would experience some horrific, gruesome *ugly*.

Does God like ugly? I don't know. But I do know a few things.

I do know that God IS a God of justice, mercy, and unfailing love.

I know that God's justice does not look like our justice because God does not judge the way that we judge.

I know that what we may see as *ugly,* God sees as raw material (potential).

I know God sees value where we may not.

I know God can take *ugly* things and revalue, repurpose, and redeem them as beautiful.

I know He did it for my mother.

I know He has done it for me.

I know He can do it for you!

> Do you have some ugliness in your life? Put it in Master's hands and let Him create something brand new and beautiful with it. *(Revelation 21:5)*

Would you allow Jesus to redeem the *ugliness* in your life? He can do it. He's willing to do it. He wants to do it. He's waiting to do it! Let Him in! Let Jesus show you His redemptive nature and bring something beautiful out of your ugliness. Allow Him to resurrect your dead situations, relationships, hopes, dreams, and joy just like He Resurrected from an ugly death. Allow Him to show you the true value of what you are worth to Him? You're priceless! Let the Redeemer show you just HOW priceless!

CHAPTER 5

Let Go and Let God

By: Minister Jeanette Lebron

Introduction

"Let go and let God." This simple, five-word phrase has become a cornerstone of contemporary Christian language. It's emblazoned on coffee mugs, embroidered on throw pillows, and painted on decorative wooden signs that hang in countless Christian homes. The phrase is often offered as sage advice to those struggling with anxiety, depression, uncertainty, or situations beyond their control. Yet, like many popular Christian adages, this phrase deserves deeper scrutiny. Does it accurately reflect biblical teaching? Or, like other well-meaning but potentially misleading phrases, does it offer an oversimplified approach to faith that may ultimately prove spiritually counterproductive?

The essence of "let go and let God" suggests surrendering our problems, plans, and control to divine guidance. On its surface, this appears wholly consistent with Christian theology—a recognition of human limitations and divine sovereignty. However, this chapter explores the nuanced biblical understanding of surrender, divine providence, and human agency that lies beneath this popular expression. We'll examine whether Scripture truly calls for passive surrender or for something more complex: an active trust that involves both yielding to God's will and participating in His work.

Be Still | *Raphah* | Let Go

I remember a time when life was so busy that I didn't even have time to think. Everything was a distraction, and if I found a free minute, it quickly became occupied with a task. My life quickly filled up like a boat retaining water, getting ready to sink. It got so bad at one point that I was losing sleep, friends, and peace of mind. I turned to a friend for help, and all she could muster up to tell me was, *"You just gotta let go and let God."* What does that look like? What am I letting go and letting God do? How was this supposed to help? I quickly turned to the Bible and found this Scripture in Psalm 46:10 NKJV: **"Be still, and know that I am God."** Did you know that the Word of God mentions being still eight times throughout the Bible? I took a step back, stopped everything, and started to re-evaluate what was important and what wasn't.

Let's dive in: Is the phrase biblical, and if so, where can I find it in the text? You won't find the phrase in the text, but several biblical passages are commonly cited as the foundation for the concept:

I was drawn to Psalm 46:10 because it calls for stillness and recognition of God's sovereignty. The Hebrew word translates as "be still" (*raphah*), which can also mean "to let go" or "to release." The psalmist writes in a context of national turmoil, calling Israel to cease striving and recognize God's authority over the nations.

So, where did the phrase come from? Despite its ubiquity in contemporary Christian culture, tracing its exact origin becomes challenging. The current popularization of the phrase likely comes from its adoption by recovery movements, particularly those addressing addiction. As Ruth Graham writes in her study "Faith in Recovery" (2012),[2] "The concept of surrendering one's will—central to addiction recovery—found natural expression in the simple directive to ‹let go and let God,' creating a bridge between therapeutic and theological understandings of surrender."

The first Scripture I ever memorized as a Believer was Proverbs 3:5-6 NKJV, "Trust in the LORD with all your heart, and lean not on your own understanding; In all your ways acknowledge Him, and He shall direct your paths." I never realized how often I would return to this Scripture over the years, but in this most recent year, I have come to understand its meaning more deeply than ever. Trusting God is an active process; you have to continually decide to allow God to be God in the moments when you're unsure. This Scripture is an explicit call to trust God rather than human wisdom, coupled with a promise of divine guidance. Biblical scholar Walter Brueggemann (2014)[3] observes that this verse is "not a suggestion for personal meditation techniques, but a radical call to faith in the midst of apparent chaos. The stillness demanded is not passive quietism but active trust in God's ordering of a disordered world."

---

2 Graham, R. (2012). Faith in recovery. [Publisher or Unpublished Manuscript]

3 Brueggemann, W. (2014). Sabbath as resistance: Saying no to the culture of now. Westminster John Knox Press.

The Lord Will Fight for You | Let God Prevail | *Tan la'elohim lehakhlit*

In 2023, I decided to "Let go and let God." I left my secure and stable job for the unknown. I wanted to walk by faith and allow God to guide my next season. Not fully understanding what I was getting myself into, I embarked on this walk that felt similar to the Israelites' departure from Egypt and their journey into the wilderness. I was reminded that Exodus 14:14, "**The LORD will fight for you; you need only to be still**," applied to me in this season. In this dramatic moment at the Red Sea, with Pharaoh's army in pursuit, Moses reassures the terrified Israelites that God will battle on their behalf while they remain still. This verse seems to embody the essence of "let go and let God." Every obstacle or moment of uncertainty was an opportunity for God to show His mighty hand. He made the impossible possible; in moments when I was unsure how I'd pay for food or gas, I simply called on His name, and the Lord provided.

However, the narrative continues with God instructing Moses in the very next verse. "Why do you cry to me? Tell the people of Israel to go forward" (Exodus 14:15, ESV). As Biblical historian William Propp (1999)[4] points out, "The divine response suggests that there are times for prayerful waiting and times for faithful action. The story presents not passive surrender but a partnership between divine power and human movement." This couldn't be truer. I would cry out to God, but God would tell me that He already gave me the tools I needed to get the job done. It was a stretching period, not only to trust

4 Propp, W. H. C. (1998). Exodus 1–18 (Anchor Yale Bible Commentaries, Vol. 2). Yale University Press.

(let go) but also to take action on what He instructed me to do and witness the miracles unfolding *(let God)*.

The phrase "Let God" in Hebrew translates a little differently. When studying deeper, the meaning expands to say **Let God Prevail** (*Rappah ve-bitach ba-El*). He is an overcomer God, the One whom we should trust, meaning that when we allow God to be the author of our situation, He always prevails. This is evidenced throughout the Bible, from the Ark to the Resurrection, where God has prevailed in every circumstance, and the people who chose to trust in Him have become the examples we read about today.

Let Go | *Ve-bitach* | Trust

Many times, the reference to "Let Go" usually follows bouts of anxiety and is a generic term to help the person release it. Jesus' teaching on anxiety in the Sermon on the Mount advises against worry, reminding listeners of God's provision for creation. The passage concludes: "**Therefore do not worry about tomorrow**, for tomorrow will worry about itself. Each day has enough trouble of its own," according to Matthew 6:25-34. I know it seems easier said than done, but I've realized that you cannot control everything, and this was a great starting point to lower the creeping anxiety. Instead of focusing on all the things I cannot control, I put my focus on what I can control. The hardest part of letting go is realizing the biggest thing you have to let go of is the illusion of control. I cannot control the weather, but I can prepare for the storm. Because I had prepared for the storm, I was equipped to handle the unexpected outcomes.

Paul instructs the Philippians: "Do not be anxious about anything, but in every situation, by prayer and petition, with thanksgiving, present your requests to God. And the peace of God, which transcends all understanding, will guard your hearts and your minds in Christ Jesus." In the same manner in preparing for stormy weather, the Lord wants us to prepare our hearts for the unexpected storms we come across. In prayer, we can *"let go"* and trust in the One who can control what we cannot. By bringing our anxieties to God, He can transform them into peace. Does He not give the garment of praise for the spirit of heaviness? When we offer up our innermost thoughts and prayers, the Lord can make something out of them.

Let's take a closer look at the tension between human action and divine control at the heart of "Let go and let God":

Abraham's Offering of Isaac (Genesis 22)

In this gripping account, Abraham demonstrates extraordinary trust by preparing to sacrifice his son in obedience to God's command. His willingness to surrender his most precious possession—indeed, the very son through whom God had promised to fulfill His covenant—exemplifies profound faith. Abraham's trust in God required not just a passive acceptance but an active decision and agonizing obedience.

The resolution of the story—God providing a ram as a substitute—comes not while Abraham is waiting idly but while he is actively carrying out God's will.

Joseph's Response to Betrayal (Genesis 37-50)

Sold into slavery by his brothers, falsely accused, and imprisoned, Joseph had every reason to become bitter. Yet the

Scripture reveals his persistent trust in God's providence, culminating in his famous statement to his brothers: "You intended to harm me, but God intended it for good" (Genesis 50:20). Joseph's unwavering faithfulness to his character in every circumstance is an example to us all.

Joseph's surrender to God's providence did not manifest as resignation to circumstance but as excellence in every role assigned to him.

Daniel's Friends in the Fiery Furnace (Daniel 3)

When Shadrach, Meshach, and Abednego refused to bow to Nebuchadnezzar's golden image, they demonstrated remarkable trust: "If we are thrown into the blazing furnace, the God we serve is able to deliver us from it... But even if he does not, we want you to know, Your Majesty, that we will not serve your gods" (Daniel 3:17-18 NIV).

This statement contains three crucial elements that illuminate the proper understanding of "let go and let God":

- First, confidence in God's ability: "God is able to deliver us." They acknowledge divine power without presuming upon it.
- Second, acceptance of God's sovereignty: "But even if he does not..." They surrender the outcome to God's wisdom without demanding a particular result.
- Third, commitment to faithful action: "We will not serve your gods." Their surrender to God manifests not as passive acceptance but as resolute disobedience to the king's ungodly command.

Mary's Response to the Angel (Luke 1:26-38)

When the angel Gabriel appeared to Mary with the news that she would bear the Messiah, her response became one of the most profound examples of surrender in Scripture: "I am the Lord's servant. May your word to me be fulfilled" (Luke 1:38). This simple statement, often called her fiat (Latin for "let it be"), exemplifies the essence of "letting go and letting God."

Yet Mary's surrender was far from passive resignation. The costly implications of her "yes" were enormous—potential rejection by Joseph, community shame, the legal penalty for apparent adultery, and the unprecedented responsibility of raising the Messiah. Her surrender led immediately to action, as Luke records: "At that time Mary got ready and hurried to a town in the hill country of Judea" (Luke 1:39) to visit Elizabeth, seeking both confirmation and support.

The Passive Trap | I Need A Sign

Several Christian thinkers have raised significant concerns about misinterpretations of the "let go and let God" mindset, particularly when it morphs into what might be called "waiting for a sign" spirituality. This passive posture toward divine guidance can become a spiritual dead end, leaving Believers paralyzed with indecision rather than empowered by faith.

Kevin DeYoung, in his insightful book "Just Do Something" (2009),[5] offers one of the most thorough critiques of this mindset: "The problem with this kind of thinking is that it makes God's will something to be discovered rather than something to be done. We are not called to passive mysticism

5 DeYoung, K. (2009). Just do something: A liberating approach to finding God's will. Moody Publishers.

but to active obedience to the clear commands of Scripture." DeYoung argues that Christians often spiritualize what are essentially ordinary decisions, creating a "holy paralysis" that impedes both personal growth and kingdom work.

Theologian R.C. Sproul echoes this concern in his work "Can I Know God's Will?" (2009),[6] writing: "We want God to reveal His will to us through signs rather than through Scripture because we would rather have Him direct us through external means than internal ones. It's easier to look for a sign than to develop wisdom and character." This insight reveals a profound spiritual laziness that can lurk behind our desire for divine billboards pointing the way forward.

When Waiting Becomes Avoidance

I am reminded of a recent situation with a friend of mine. He was unsure if he should ask one of the sisters at the church out for a date. He contemplated for months, and one day he said, "I'm just gonna wait here for a sign from God." Instead of asking God to guide his steps and to give him the words to speak, he just took the passive approach and waited and waited.

His waiting, rather than being a sign of faith, became a spiritual-sounding excuse for avoiding the vulnerability of potential rejection. For three months, he prayed for unmistakable confirmation while making no move. He scrutinized every interaction with this woman for divine hints—did her smile mean God was saying yes? Did her absence from church last Sunday signal divine disapproval? When they were coinci-

6 Sproul, R. C. (2009). Can I know God's will? (Crucial Questions Series). Reformation Trust Publishing.

dentally assigned to the same ministry team, he wondered if this was finally his "sign." This allowance for time, instead of being a period of growth and self-reflection, became a stagnant pool, delaying his personal and relational development. Imagine the growth he would have experienced, even if he was met with rejection.

What my friend failed to recognize was that God had already given him everything needed to make this decision. He had been equipped with Scripture's wisdom about godly character and relationships. He had been blessed with community discernment through trusted friends who knew both him and the woman well. He had been given a sound mind capable of weighing factors like shared values, mutual interests, and complementary life directions. Yet he bypassed all these resources, waiting instead for some dramatic divine intervention that would eliminate all risk from his decision.

Biblical Wisdom vs. Biblical Magic

Pastor and author Andy Stanley addresses this tendency in his work "The Principle of the Path" (2008)[7]: "We treat the Bible as if it were a magic book full of secret formulas rather than a wisdom book full of sound principles." This distinction between biblical wisdom and biblical magic reveals the heart of the issue. Scripture primarily teaches us how to develop discernment and character rather than providing on-demand answers to life's specific decisions.

When "let go and let God" devolves into waiting for signs, we often practice what Old Testament scholar John Walton

7 Stanley, A. (2008). The Principle of the Path: How to get from where you are to where you want to be. Thomas Nelson.

calls "spiritual divination"—attempting to manipulate or decode God's will through external signs rather than developing spiritual maturity. This approach more closely resembles ancient pagan practices than biblical faith.

The Gideon Exception

Can God provide a sign? Absolutely. He did it with Gideon in Judges; however, Gideon repeatedly questioned God's promises and constantly needed reassurance that God was with him. As New Testament scholar Craig Keener observes in "Gift and Giver" (2001)[8]: "Gideon's fleece was not a model for Christian decision-making but rather a concession to Gideon's weak faith. Throughout Scripture, God consistently moves His people toward greater maturity, not more signs."

The narrative context of Gideon's story is crucial for proper interpretation. God had already clearly revealed His will to Gideon through direct communication. The "fleece tests" represent Gideon's reluctance to trust what God had already plainly stated, not a normative model for seeking guidance. Old Testament theologian Daniel Block notes in "Judges, Ruth" (1999)[9] that "the story presents Gideon's requests for signs as expressions of doubt rather than exemplars of faith."

Furthermore, as a child of God, we know that the Lord is with us. This fundamental promise of divine presence—"I am with you always, to the end of the age" (Matthew 28:20 NIV)—provides a foundation for confident action rather than anxious waiting. New Testament scholar Scot McKnight writes in "The

---

8 Keener, C. S. (2001). Gift and giver: The Holy Spirit for today. Baker Academic.

9 Block, D. I. (1999). Judges, Ruth: An Exegetical Theological Exposition of Holy Scripture (The New American Commentary Series, Vol. 6). B&H Publishing Group.

Letter of James" (2011)[10]: "The certainty of God's presence liberates us from sign-seeking and frees us for faithful action."

Let Go and Let God Prevail

"Let go and let God" encapsulates a profound spiritual truth—our need to surrender control and trust divine providence. Yet, like many popular Christian phrases, it risks oversimplification if taken as a complete theology rather than a situational reminder.

Biblical faith calls not for passive resignation but for active trust—what theologian Dietrich Bonhoeffer called "costly discipleship." I am reminded in Luke 14:28 that it is important to count the cost before you build or risk not having enough to finish. This cost can be time, relationships, and work. We are invited to release our anxiety, surrender our self-sufficiency, and trust God's sovereignty while simultaneously embracing our responsibility to act faithfully within God's will.

Augustine's wisdom strikes the appropriate balance: "Pray as though everything depended on God. Work as though everything depended on you." This paradoxical approach better captures the biblical tension between divine sovereignty and human responsibility than any five-word slogan could.

As we navigate life's challenges, Scripture invites us neither to anxious self-reliance nor to passive fatalism, but to faithful participation in God's ongoing work. We are called not merely to "let go and let God" but to "trust God and take responsibility"—surrendering outcomes while embracing obedience,

10 McKnight, Scot. (2011). The Letter of James (Part of Series: The New International Commentary on the New Testament (NICNT)). Eerdmans.

releasing anxiety while engaging in challenges, and acknowledging limits while exercising agency.

In this more nuanced understanding, we find not just a catchy phrase but a sustainable spirituality—one that honors both divine sovereignty and human responsibility, that values both prayerful waiting and faithful action, and that embraces both receiving grace and responding to it. This is the way of Jesus, who both surrendered to the Father's will in Gethsemane and actively embraced the cross at Calvary.

From the time I gave my life to Christ till now, I've learned the true meaning of letting God direct my paths. I remember vividly the paralysis I once felt at life's crossroads—frozen in decision-making, fearing whether each choice aligned with God's perfect plan. Every decision became a spiritual crisis: Was this God's will or my own? Was I stepping out in faith or presumption? This anxiety masked itself as spiritual sensitivity, but in reality, it revealed a fundamental misunderstanding of how divine guidance operates in Believers' lives. I always thought that if my decision wasn't in the will of God, then He wouldn't allow it, but that's not the case. Sometimes, you need to make the decision, and God begins to reveal His will in your life. Deciding to leave a stable career to become an entrepreneur was a moment of stepping out in faith. I was not sure if this decision was in God's will, but I had to trust that He would be my provider. It's been 3 years since that decision and I have never been in lack.

The transformation came not through a dramatic revelation but through the gentle unfolding of Scripture's wisdom in everyday experience. Proverbs 16:9 (NIV) became living truth for me: "In their hearts humans plan their course, but the LORD establishes their steps." I began to understand that God's sovereignty operates not despite my decisions but through them. I went from being frozen in decision-making to trusting that God would be there every step of the way, guiding and correcting me along the way.

This shift fundamentally changed my approach to Christian living. Rather than anxiously awaiting unmistakable signs before moving forward, I learned to walk in faithful obedience to what Scripture commands, trusting God with the outcomes of decisions made with the wisdom He provides.

This testimony echoes what the Psalmist discovered: "The LORD makes firm the steps of the one who delights in him; though he may stumble, he will not fall, for the LORD upholds him with his hand" (Psalm 37:23-24 NIV). The promise is not an exemption from missteps but divine presence through them all—the ultimate expression of what it truly means to "let go and let God."

CHAPTER 6
Just Keep the Faith

By: Minister Patsy Hill

Keeping the Faith: A Christian Perspective

Faith is the foundation of Christianity. It is an unwavering trust in God's promises, a conviction in the unseen, and an assurance of things hoped for (Hebrews 11:1). Keeping the faith is a journey that involves trials, refinement, and steadfastness. As Believers, our faith is tested and validated through life's trials, refining us like gold in fire (1 Peter 1:7). In this chapter, I will begin with a prayer of salvation. Then, I will explore the importance of faith, its role in Christian living, and the significance of trusting in God's promises. Finally, I will share a bit of my personal testimony as it relates to growing in faith.

We must have faith and understand what Christian faith truly is. Anything you read in the pages of this book will mean absolutely nothing to you if you do not grasp the essence of the Christian faith. However, before we can even discuss faith, I must invite you into a relationship with the Lord because, without Him, nothing is possible. I know this to be true in my life. I tried doing life without God at the center, and I was a hot mess! But once I submitted and gave my life to Christ and began discovering who He really is, it changed my life, and I will never return to a life devoid of Christ. Therefore, I would like to start with a prayer of salvation, and we will move forward from there.

You may wonder why I need to start with a prayer of salvation. When we talk about the Salvation Prayer or "The Sinner's Prayer," we're referring to a heartfelt plea to God in which a person expresses belief in God's salvation through Jesus, repents of their sins, and asks Him to forgive them and be the Lord of their lives. This prayer is a pivotal moment, marking the beginning of a changed life. A personal relationship with Christ is the gateway to true faith. A personal relationship with God has always been His plan for us.

Scripture tells us that in the beginning, God intentionally created the heavens and the earth with beauty and purpose. Everything He made was good (Genesis 1:31), reflecting His character and glory. Humanity, made in His image (Genesis 1:27), was placed in the garden to enjoy creation and engage in close fellowship with the Creator. God's original plan envisioned humankind living harmoniously with Him, stewarding the earth, and thriving under His loving reign. There was no death or suffering, only peace, joy, and God's presence. However, following the fall in Genesis 3, sin entered the world, distorting that original plan. Yet, abundant in mercy, God quickly set His redemptive plan in motion. From the promise of a Savior who would defeat the serpent (Genesis 3:15) to the covenant with Abraham and the coming of Christ, God never abandoned His purpose. His original plan is unchanged but fulfilled in Christ, who reconciles all things to Himself (Colossians 1:19–20). The ultimate goal is a renewed creation where God once again dwells with His people (Revelation 21:3–5).

I invite those who have not yet accepted Christ, as well as those who wish to reaffirm their relationship with Him, to pray the following prayer:

If you would like to join me in a prayer of salvation, please read the following prayer aloud:

"Lord Jesus, I repent of my sins and surrender my life. Wash me clean. I believe that Jesus Christ is the Son of God. That He died on the cross for my sins and rose again on the third day for my Victory. I believe in my heart and confess with my mouth that Jesus is my Savior and Lord. In Jesus' name, I pray, Amen!

Romans 10:9-10 states, "If you declare with your mouth, "Jesus is Lord," and believe in your heart that God raised him from the dead, you will be saved. For it is with your heart that you believe and are justified, and it is with your mouth that you profess your faith and are saved."

What is the meaning and importance of faith? I'm glad you asked. At its core, faith is trust in God's Word and sovereignty. The Bible defines faith as "the substance of things hoped for, the evidence of things not seen" (Hebrews 11:1). Without faith, it is impossible to please God (Hebrews 11:6). It is more than just a belief; it is a lifestyle. Jesus emphasized the power of faith when He said, "According to your faith, let it be done to you" (Matthew 9:29). Faith enables Believers to receive God's promises and live a life that reflects His glory.

The testing of faith is a crucial aspect of spiritual growth. James 1:2-3 encourages Believers to "consider it pure joy when you face trials of many kinds because you know that the testing of your faith produces perseverance." This perseverance, born out of faith, is a powerful tool in the face of adversity. Trials refine faith, removing impurities and strengthening reliance on God. In 1 Peter 1:7, faith is compared to gold tested by fire, signifying its value and the necessity of refinement. Paul also warns Timothy against distractions that lead away from true faith, urging him to hold firm to the doctrine (1 Timothy 1:4). By holding onto faith, Believers stand resilient against doubts and trials, maintaining their commitment to God's truth.

Walking by faith requires trusting God beyond what is visible. 2 Corinthians 5:7 states, "For we walk by faith, not by sight." Abraham exemplifies this kind of faith. In Genesis 15:6, Abraham "believed the Lord, and He credited it to him as righteousness." His unwavering trust in God's promise is an example for Believers today. Jesus also spoke about the power of faith, saying, "If you have faith as small as a mustard seed, you can say to this mountain, ‹Move from here to there,' and it will move" (Matthew 17:20). This powerful statement should inspire us, reminding us that even the smallest faith can bring about great miracles when placed in God's hands. We should learn to walk by faith by applying the Word of God and standing on it, not complacent but consistent in the waiting as we grow in our faith. Our strength comes in waiting on the Lord. Isaiah 40:28-31 states, "Do you not know? Have you not heard? The Everlasting God, the Lord, the Creator of the ends of the earth, does not become weary or tired. His understanding is inscrutable. He gives strength to the weary, and to him who lacks might, He increases power. Though youths grow weary and tired, And vigorous young men stumble badly, Yet those who wait for the Lord will gain new strength; They will mount up with wings like eagles, They will run and not get tired, They will walk and not become weary."

Many people mistakenly believe that gaining power comes from quickening our pace. In reality, it involves slowing down, staying centered on God, seeking His guidance, and asking for His strength to fulfill our divine purpose. There's no earthly explanation for what God can do through a surrendered person. His Holy Spirit moves like a potent, refreshing breeze, allowing us to rise like eagles (Psalm 103:5). When you feel exhausted, pause to refocus on the Lord. Are you in harmony with Him, or have you rushed ahead? Align your speed with His. Allow yourself time to rest when He calls for it, and welcome the strength He abundantly gives to those who walk in obedience to His will, in His perfect timing.

How does the role of trust and hope in faith work in our lives? Faith is inseparable from trust and hope. Trusting God means believing in His plans even when circumstances seem dire. Proverbs 3:5-6 instructs Believers to "trust in the Lord with all your heart and lean not on your own understanding." Hope fuels faith, giving Believers the confidence that God's promises will come to pass. Paul emphasizes the connection between faith and salvation in Romans 10:9-10, declaring that confessing Jesus as Lord and believing in His resurrection leads to salvation. Faith is not just about believing but about trusting God with one's entire being.

Living by faith requires daily trust in God's will. Romans 4:9 speaks of Abraham's faith being credited as righteousness, reinforcing that faith leads to a righteous life. As Believers, faith should guide our decisions, actions, and interactions. James 1:6 warns against doubt, stating, "The one who doubts is like a wave of the sea, blown and tossed by the wind." Doubt weakens faith, hindering spiritual growth. To remain strong in faith, Believers must immerse themselves in God's Word, prayer, and fellowship with other Christians.

At times, I wonder if I am being complacent or consistent; I'm not sure. Throughout my journey with the Lord, I've learned the importance of consistency in my faith. This understanding led me to write this chapter and share part of my story with you. For the record, never in a million years would I have thought I would participate in writing a book. To be honest with you, I was not overjoyed to participate in the endeavor. First, I am not a writer, and I thank God for spell check because I can't spell to save my life. Second, what do I have to share with God's people that is relevant and anointed by God? Lastly, I feel that inadequacy sometimes comes over me when teaching or sharing God's Word. I always question, did I say it the way you wanted me to, Lord? Should I have explained in more detail? This may sound trivial to some, but to me, our Father in Heaven is my everything. I take every assignment He bestows on me with the utmost humility, praying that I can accomplish the assignment in the spirit of excellence.

After receiving the offer to write a chapter from a fellow ministry classmate, let me Tell You…I laughed so hard. I was like, yeah, that sounds like me NOT! In fact, I'd typed and later deleted an email saying it was not for me. A whole week passed, and I didn't think any more about it. Then, one day, I was doing some research for a class I attended. Clear as day, I heard "Patsy write the chapter for the book." I ignored it and kept working on what I was doing. Later, I was driving, and I heard it again. So, being the Christian I am, I said I got to pray about this like God wasn't speaking to me already. You can laugh if you want to, but I know I am not the only one who does this when God tells them something they don't want to hear. At times, we process what we hear as if the message is intended for somebody but not us. All joking aside, I prayed about writing the chapter for the book and immediately received the same response. I would love to say I immediately reached out to my former classmate with a resounding yes, but that was not the case. Instead, I attempted to convince God that I was not the person for this assignment. I explained to Him how I was back in college and my other responsibilities, and that I don't think I can do it. He let me finish and said to write the chapter. I said, 'Okay.' What do I write? He told me to tell my story, so here I am, sharing my story with you and demonstrating that I am still a work in progress. I am constantly walking in faith.

> *"Faith is taking the first step even when you don't see the whole staircase (Martin Luther King Jr.)."*[11]

Keeping the faith has impacted my life. In 2017, my pastor and mentor approached me after one of our Thursday night classes, asking if I was ready to be stretched a little further. At first, I almost opened my mouth to say yes, but I paused because the smile on her face was slightly different. So, I

11 Attributed to Martin Luther King Jr., in Marable and Mullings, Let Nobody Turn Us Around, 202.

replied, "How?" She said with the biggest smile she had ever given me that I would be facilitating one of the breakout sessions at the upcoming retreat.

I was in shock, nearly speechless. I thought my mentor might ask me to stand in for some of her other duties. I looked at her, and she was still beaming at me. My brain finally caught up; she was waiting for my response. I blurted, "You think I'm ready for that?" Lord, she thinks I'm ready for that? Lord, do you think I'm ready for that?" And, of course, she was still smiling at me. I asked, "Can I think about it?" She answered, "Of course you can," while masking a look of panic on my face. I inquired about the topic I would be speaking on. She calmly responded that I would be discussing standing on the Lord's Word.

After leaving class, I prayed and asked God whether I should speak at the retreat during the drive home. Immediately, I received the word "yes." But I told myself, "No, I didn't hear that," so I went home. I prayed a few more times about what to do that week, trying to change how I asked the question as if I could trick God. His answer was the same. Do you see my pattern here when God gives me an answer I don't want? I told you I'm a work in progress; I am better now than I was at this time in my life. The following week, I told her I would be honored to speak at the retreat, despite having no idea what I would talk about for 45 minutes.

Meanwhile, my spiritual life was growing, and I sought to know more of the Lord. Every other aspect of my life was falling apart. I had worked at my job for twenty years and continued to face issues daily, but I wouldn't quit. I thought maybe that was how I was standing on the Word of God, trusting Him to get me through this. I didn't realize that I was being complacent in my thinking because, unbeknownst to me, a turn of events was about to take place in my life. I was not ready for the events that were about to unfold. I lost my job, one of my children was contemplating suicide, and to top it all off, my husband decided to accept a job offer overseas. I felt broken and like I was a failure in those three areas of my life as a mother, wife, and registered nurse. I was hurting, and no one around me could see it. I know the people around me meant well when they would say things like: you just got to keep the faith; God doesn't give us more than we can handle; when one door closes, another one opens, or my favorite, you are a nurse you can quit a job today and get another today. My sense of identity, of who I thought I was, crumbled all around me.

> *"Anytime God calls us to die,*
> *His purpose is to reveal larger life*
> —Beth Moore"[12]

I agreed to speak at the retreat in less than three weeks. I had three weeks to prepare, and I had nothing to share. With all the drama going on in my personal and professional life, coupled with grieving the loss I perceived at the time, I just didn't feel worthy. However, since I had promised my mentor I would speak, I wanted to keep my word. I began praying, asking the Lord for guidance on what direction to take with the broad topic of faith. Oh, by the way, I was still praying every

12 Moore, B. (1999). Breaking free: Discover the victory of total surrender. LifeWay Press.

day, asking why He let this happen to me, basically crying and mourning the things I perceived I lost. The Lord answered my prayer, giving me the following Scriptures:

1. **Standing in Faith (1 Timothy 3:13).**

   Those who have served well gain an excellent standing and great assurance in their Faith in Christ Jesus.

2. **Walking by faith (2 Corinthians 5:7).**

   For we walk by faith, not by sight.

3. **Moving from glory to glory (2 Corinthians 3:18).**

   But we all, with unveiled faces, beholding as in a mirror the glory of the Lord, are being transformed into the same image from glory to glory, just as by the Spirit of the Lord.

4. **Maturity (Hebrews 6:1).**

   Therefore, let us move beyond the elementary teachings about Christ and be taken forward to maturity, not laying again the foundation of repentance from acts that lead to death and of Faith in God.

5. **Being Bold and courageous (1 Corinthians 16:13).**

   Be on your guard; stand firm in the faith; be courageous; be strong.

6. **Being consistent, not complacent (1 Corinthians 15:58).**

   Therefore, my dear brothers and sisters, stand firm. Let nothing move you. Always give yourselves fully to the work of the Lord because you know that your labor in the Lord is not in vain.

7. **People pleasing is a snare (Galatians 1:10).**

   Am I now trying to win the approval of human beings or of God? Or am I trying to please people? If I were still trying to please people, I would not be a servant of Christ.

8. **Staying steadfast (Isaiah 26:3).**

   You will keep in perfect peace those whose minds are steadfast because they trust in you.

9. **God is always working things in my favor (Romans 8:28).**

   And we know that in all things, God works for the good of those who love him, who have been called according to his purpose.

10. **John 6:5-6.**

    When Jesus looked up and saw a great crowd coming toward him, he said to Philip, "Where shall we buy bread for these people to eat?

    He asked this only to test him, for he already knew what he would do. He said everyone is tested, and it's how you respond that matters. Philip saw with his eyes that Jesus had healed and calmed the sea, but he doubted that Jesus could feed the crowd. Where was his Faith?

11. **James 1:3.**

    Because you know that the testing of your faith produces perseverance.

12. **James 2:14-23.**

    What good is it, my brothers and sisters, if someone claims to have faith but has no deeds? Can such faith save them? Suppose a brother or a sister is without clothes and daily

> food. If one of you says to them, "Go in peace; keep warm and well fed," but does nothing about their physical needs, what good is it? In the same way, faith by itself, if it is not accompanied by action, is dead. But someone will say, "You have faith; I have deeds." Show me your faith without deeds, and I will show you my faith by my deeds. You believe that there is one God. Good! Even the demons believe that and shudder. You foolish person, do you want evidence that faith without deeds is useless? Was not our father Abraham considered righteous for what he did when he offered his son Isaac on the altar? You see that his faith and his actions were working together, and his faith was made complete by what he did. And the scripture was fulfilled that says, "Abraham believed God, and it was credited to him as righteousness," and he was called God's friend.

I studied these Scriptures and prepared a message for the retreat. While studying, I realized the message was for myself: I needed to stand on my faith in God. Have you ever been so busy looking for the lesson that you missed the lesson? He was growing me, testing and refining me, and strengthening me. I showed up at the retreat ready to share everything the Lord shared with me. I was so nervous that I felt my body shaking. How would I speak if I can't get these shakes under control? We prayed for all the speakers who would be speaking at the retreat. When it was my time to talk, I stood before the people, praying before I began. I shared two points of the message I worked on before the Holy Spirit took over. I was but a mere vessel, transformed by the power of faith.

Weeks after the retreat, I decided to start volunteering in my administrative capacity at the church, leading more classes, and taking classes. One thing led to another, and before I knew it, I was enrolled in ministry school, graduated, and at the time of writing this book, I am currently in a theology program that I will finish in the spring of 2026. I don't know what God has in store for my future, but I trust and have Faith in Him; nevertheless, His will be done, not mine.

> *"Optimism is the faith that leads to achievement. Nothing can be done without hope and confidence"*
> —Helen Keller[13]

My hope rests firmly in the unwavering glory of Christ, who has redeemed me and is also making all things new. In a world marked by brokenness, I draw strength from the truth that Jesus, the radiance of God's glory (Hebrews 1:3), is the Author and Finisher of my faith (Hebrews 12:2). His resurrection power reassures me that sin and death do not have the final word. I look forward to the day I will see Him face to face. Until then, I live with confident hope. As Paul states, "Our present sufferings are not worth comparing to the glory that will be revealed in us" (Romans 8:18). Christ in me represents the hope of glory (Colossians 1:27), and that hope fuels my journey. It enables me to live faithfully, love courageously, and face challenges with joy, knowing that what lies ahead is far greater than what we experience now.

I don't have any secret steps or insights to share with you on how to be consistent, have faith, or stand on the Word of the

13 Keller, H. (1903). Optimism: An essay. T.Y. Crowell & Co.

Lord. However, I can suggest that you trust in Him, and build a relationship with Him by reading His Word and spending time with Him. Keeping the faith is a lifelong journey of trusting God, persevering through trials, and walking in His promises. The Bible repeatedly emphasizes the power of faith, from Abraham's unwavering trust to Jesus' teachings on faith's ability to move mountains. As Believers, we are called to live by faith, anchored in the assurance of God's Word. By holding firm to faith, we draw closer to God and experience His transformative power in our lives. All we have to do is be obedient and walk by faith, trusting in the Lord without borders or boundaries!

This is the sound of my trumpet!

CHAPTER 7
God Gives You the Desires of Your Heart

By: Minister Erin Achane

"Delight thyself also in the Lord: and he shall give thee the desires of thine heart." —Psalm 37:4 KJV

"Therefore I say unto you, What things soever ye desire, when ye pray, believe that ye receive them, and ye shall have them." —Mark 11:24 KJV

For most of my life, I've had a distorted image of who God was. When I was a child in Christ, I thought as a child. I couldn't understand this God I could not see, so I squared Him up with things I could see. I thought God was like Santa Claus, living in the North Pole, a place that I could not see but just had to believe existed. I thought he had a naughty and a nice list, and if you were on the 'nice' list, only good things would happen to you, but if you were on the 'naughty' list, you wouldn't get what you asked for. Then I found out Santa wasn't real, and God was way more complex than in a red suit. I later evolved into thinking God was like the genie in the movie Aladdin. He was hanging out in the clouds, just waiting for me to rub his lamp so he could grant me three wishes. So there was no way he was wearing a red suit, fitting in a lamp, or a wizard. I even thought God was like the Wiz. Not the *Wizard of Oz,* but the Wiz who lived in Oz. But then it dawned on me that the Wiz was just Richard Pryor! And the Wiz had no real power; he was just an ordinary man. But I heard my grandmother say the Lord was the creator of all things.

I attempted to compare him with something I could understand. I needed to be able to rationalize God without truly knowing him. I went to church as a kid, and depending on what type of church you grew up in, it shaped your image of God. I grew up Baptist, then turned COGIC, and I heard the Word, but truly didn't understand it. I was saved but never disciplined. I had the basics, but since my understanding of God's character was so limited, I took this segment of Scripture, *"God Gives You the Desires of Your Heart,"* out of context for years.

To attempt to understand the Word, you must have a factual understanding of God's nature. There is nothing that ever was, that is, or will ever be that can compare to God! God is so vast, so grand, so extraordinary that any comparison falls short. He is Eternal, which means He was never born and will never die. He is sovereign, which means he answers to nobody. He does what he pleases. He knows every detail about every creature, dead or alive, past, present, and future.

In his book "The Attributes of God," A.W. Pink[14] says, "God is self-contained, independent, and is separate from all other creatures."

Everything that exists only exists because He willed it so!

---

14 Pink, A. W. (2006). The Attributes of God. Baker Books. Republication.

Exodus 15:11 (KJV) states:

> *"Who is like unto thee, O LORD, among the gods? who is like thee, glorious in holiness, fearful in praises, doing wonders? "*

In the beginning was God. Before He created heaven or the earth, there was God. If you can go as far back as your mind can take you, God was there. Standing there, perfectly content within and in need of nothing.

> *"He gives to all. But needs nothing. Unique in his Excellency. Sustains all. But independent of all. Such a God can not be found, but revealed by the Holy Spirit."*
> —A.W. Pink

Everything God made was made outside of time. His decrees are absolute and unconditional. By speaking the word, everything came into existence. He knows events in heaven, on earth, and in hell. Nothing is hidden from Him; his knowledge exceeds all our human understanding.

> *"You have searched me, LORD, and you know me.*
> *You know when I sit and when I rise; you perceive my thoughts from afar. You discern my going out and my lying down; you are familiar with all my ways, Before a word is on my tongue you, LORD, know it completely. You hem me in behind and before, and you lay your hand upon me.*
> *Such knowledge is too wonderful for me,*
> *too lofty for me to attain."*
> *—Psalm 139:1-6 NIV*

It is important to discuss the character of God, as without it, we will read Scripture and distort it to fit our perspective rather than God's intention.

God created the whole world and set it perfectly in place. And once the scene was set, He created us, mankind, to have dominion over it. He placed Adam and Eve in the garden and gave Adam one simple command: don't eat from the Tree of the Knowledge of Good and Evil. But Satan tricked Eve, she ate, and then Adam followed. They disobeyed God, and because of that, sin entered the world and spread through Adam's seed to every generation. From that moment on, we were born into a curse we didn't choose, but God's love never stopped chasing us. He could've left us there, but instead, He made a plan to bring us back. All throughout the Old Testament, God kept reaching out, sending judges, kings, and prophets to guide His people. But none of it could save us. We needed a Savior. And because God loved us so much, He sent Jesus, born of a virgin, not from man's seed, but by the Holy Spirit. Jesus took the punishment we deserved. He stood in our place and reversed the curse that started all the way back in Genesis.

Now that we have a better understanding of God's unlimited power and his love for us, let's take a look at this verse with a fresh perspective.

The issue with the text is that we are thinking about it in the wrong order. We need to reverse it. It's not that God will give you whatever you desire, but the truth is, the things you desire, He gave to you. If you are saved, the desires you have are not yours; they came from Him! He places the desires in your heart. That changes the game. I desire to be a good mom; God gave me that desire. I desire to be a good wife; He gave me that desire, too. I desire to make people feel important, seen, and valued. That's God working in me, giving me desires I didn't have before.

The closer we draw to God, the more He replaces desires that sprang from our sinful nature with new desires born out of fellowship with Him, aligning with His purpose for our lives. And you can grow closer to nurture your relationship with the Lord in so many ways. Praying, worshiping, reading the Word, and spending alone time in His presence is a must! I'll prove it. If you are reading this book, it's because you have a curiosity about God, or you want to deepen your relationship with God. Your desire is not an accident. I don't care if your aunt gave you this book to read; she knows, and so do I, that God chose you first. To say you chose Him first, and that's why he chose you, is contradictory to His Sovereign, All-Powerful, All-Knowing Godship. Like we took God by surprise with our decision to be saved? We're late! God knew since the beginning of time.

> *"For he chose us in him before the creation of the world to be holy and blameless in his sight. In love he predestined us for adoption to sonship through Jesus Christ, in accordance with his pleasure and will to the praise of his glorious grace, which he has freely given us in the One he loves."*
> *—Ephesians 1:4-5 NKJV*

You can also check the Book of Jeremiah.

> *"The Word of the Lord came to me, saying, 'Before I formed you in the womb I knew you, before you were born I set you apart; I appointed you as a prophet to the nations.'"*
> *—Jeremiah 1:4-5 NKJV*

"We love because he first loved us."
—1 John 4:19 NKJV

I need to make it clear. Not all desires come from God. If you are currently desiring somebody else's husband, God did not give you that! That's your flesh. So, how do you discern which desires are from God?

You have to hold your desires up against God's Word and his character. Ask yourself, does this desire "look like God?" This is important because the desires in your heart have a direct line to your mind, influencing your actions, similar to a device's IP address. As Believers, we must get to know God for ourselves. He reveals Himself to us through His Word by the Holy Spirit. Revelation about who God is has nothing to do with how smart you are, how you look, your mistakes, your parents, where you live, or what you do. It's not on the surface. It's much deeper. Revelation comes from hearing. Once you hear the Word, know the Word. If you believe and seek Him, He will most definitely reveal Himself to you. No cap!

He knows you and loves you and will make it plain so you can receive it. The Scripture says, "Delight yourself in the Lord," which means to find pleasure in the Lord, be satisfied in the Lord, find enjoyment in the Lord, and be tender toward the Lord. Then, He will give you the desires of your heart.

In Mark, we use the last sentence of that Scripture, but we don't read what came before it. Anytime a verse starts with *therefore,* we need to go back and read the preceding text.

> *"Verily I say unto you, That whosoever shall say unto this mountain, Be thou removed, and be thou cast into the sea; and shall not doubt in his heart, but shall believe that those things which he saith shall come to pass; he shall have whatsoever he saith. Therefore I say unto you, What things soever ye desire, when ye pray, believe that ye receive them, and ye shall have them. And when ye stand praying, forgive, if ye have ought against any: that your Father also which is in heaven may forgive you your trespasses."*
> *—Mark 23-25 KJV*

So, this verse has some conditions attached that we must follow in order to get the desired part. He says we must believe that it will be done. That's faith. It says, and when you pray, forgive others so God can forgive you. Our culture is stuck on, "I'll forgive but I'll never forget." Unforgiveness hinders your prayers. Sometimes it is not somebody else we need to forgive but our own selves. We can't walk into the promises of God, the new thing He wants to do in us, if we keep looking back. I heard a pastor say, If we don't kill who we used to be, that old person will kill who you are supposed to be.

When we died in Christ, that old person died. We were born again. You are still yourself, just that the moves you make now, and the decisions you make, are rooted in God. When I was younger, I used to fight a lot. But now, instead of throwing bows after the club, I am throwing bows at the devil. As a teenager growing up in South Louisiana, my Creole heritage, hazel eyes, and light skin had me so sassy and conceited that I stayed getting popped! Because of something that was totally out of my control, the Creole side of me is my dominant trait. I believe that because I was pretty, my life would automatically be easier. I learned that being cute may open some doors, but it's what's on the inside that will keep you in the building! God broke that pride in me and brought me to my knees! But I kept a sassy mouth. Now I'm sassy for Jesus! Same personality, but now we must use it to advance what God is doing in the Kingdom of God. We must use that oil that He has anointed us with for something bigger than just ourselves.

When I say, "Does it look like God?" this question would require you to know what He looks like. When I get a desire that was not there before, like when He gave me a desire to open a business. That idea just popped up outta thin air. I knew it was Him because where do they do that at around here? Nobody in my family had a business. Everybody I know is living paycheck to paycheck. I didn't even know anybody with a business who could mentor me on where to start. I trusted God. I knew it was Him because it wasn't me! It was too "good." It was such a great idea! The lightbulb would just flick on! I had gone to school to be a Medical Assistant. But God has people in place ready to fulfill the purpose they play in your life. Teachers mid-semester asked me to switch from Medical Assistant to Medical Billing & Coding. I didn't even know what that was! I never heard of that before. I finished school with Medical Billing and Coding, and was working on my job for only a year, and he told me to quit and start my own business, not go back to school for business. No, that would make sense, right? Nope, start the business, now. Wait! What? I started a business in a field that I had never even heard of two years prior! After 11 years, Achane Medical Billing is stronger than ever! That desire did not originate in me. It was designed for me by God, but I didn't truly know it was from him until I started walking toward it.

At that time in my life, I was saved—I was dating God. I treated him like my sugar daddy. I would only call on God when I was in trouble, which was all the time. That season in my life was the "Keith Sweat" season of my life. I was always begging, Lord please let this debit card go through! I'll pay the overdraft fees on Friday when I get paid. Or Lord, please don't let this cop search my car! I smoked a lot of weed back then, and so I just knew it was the devil trying to get me to quit my job! And to all my very holy saints reading this chapter, Yes, the Lord still spoke to me even though I would smoke on the weekends! Shocking, right?! Did I mention he was Sovereign? He knew he would deliver me from that. He was talking to the person I was going to be, not punishing me for who I was in that season. Even with the addiction, I still trusted him! I knew something bigger than myself was calling me to help doctors in a special way! I could not tell if it was God calling me to step out on faith or if I was about to make a fool of myself, but I took the leap of faith.

> *"Now faith is confidence in what we hope for and assurance about what we do not see." —Hebrews 11:1 NIV*

But this desire, this feeling of starting my own business, would not leave me alone. So I prayed to God. I praised him for being so good to me and asked him to forgive my sins. I started listing all my sins, asking him to forgive me for stuff I knew I had already asked for forgiveness for, but was still doing, and I found myself crying one of them ugly cries. I was so exhausted afterwards, and I forgot to ask him my question and just went on to get the kids ready for bed. In the midst of my regular, mundane routine, He disrupted it and whispered to me.

"Babygirl, this is what you prayed for! Go for it, I will be with you."

I immediately got into a disagreement with Him because I did not ask Him to give me my own business. I asked Him to help me take care of my kids! But when we pray, we ask for a tree, and God gives us one seed that grows into a forest if we trust Him and walk by faith.

The medical billing company is the foundation of the two other businesses I've opened up in my career, all specializing in Medicaid patients with transportation and with the primary care clinic. I've used it as a cornerstone to open several other businesses, and they all allow me to show God's love, mercy, and forgiveness to everyday people outside of the pulpit—from my employees to the people we serve. That's the Body of Christ. I know God is faithful! When you have a desire, spend time with the Holy Spirit to check if it aligns with the Word of God. If so, move toward it. Start walking in that direction by faith. Start applying to the school, start making connections outside of your circle, start looking into marketing, and start walking the desire as if it is already yours. As you get close to it, doors will open up and you can walk through to the next step. The steps of a good man are ordered. He will order your steps. When it's God, it will work out. Not because you're so awesome, but because your desire is connected to His purpose.

Now, there were times when I walked toward it, got real close, and the door didn't open. This is where we get lost. When things do not go the way we thought. When our desires that we thought came from God lead us to a dead end. This is when a lot of us give up on the desire, give up on the dream, give up on our purpose, and even give up on God.

It's a dark place because, for a moment, we stop believing. We start to doubt ourselves, and we start to doubt God. But those moments are the very moments that define your faith. Everybody's faith must be tested. It's easy to believe in God when he is your "Yes Man," your Santa Claus. But can you hold on to your faith when life pimp-slaps you across the face?!

The Bible says that the just shall walk by faith and not by sight.

Apostle Paul wrote in Romans 4:18-21 (NIV):

> *"Against all hope, Abraham in hope believed and so became the father of many nations, just as it had been said to him, ‹So shall your offspring be.' Without weakening in his faith, he faced the fact that his body was as good as dead—since he was about a hundred years old—and that Sarah's womb was also dead. Yet he did not waver through unbelief regarding the promise of God, but was strengthened in his faith and gave glory to God, being fully persuaded that God had power to do what he had promised. This is why 'it was credited to him as righteousness.'"*

Abraham had every reason to give up on the purpose God made him. God promised him he would be the father of many nations. How could that promise come to pass if he didn't have any children? Naturally, it wasn't looking good. Abraham was old, and so was Sarah. But Abraham held on to his faith, and through that season, his faith was strengthened. God kept his promises to Abraham by giving him Isaac. God counted him as righteous because he held on to his faith. What made him righteous was the fact that he believed God would do it. God had promised him! I know the situation looked impossible, but did I mention God is All Powerful? God is not stunting biological clocks or laws of gravity or any other "laws" we hold as truth. This is the same God who opened the Red Sea, and the children of Israel walked across on dry land! Who does that? The Lord of Heaven's Armies.

In those seasons, the best way to hold on to your faith is to hold on to your worship. Hold fast to your praise! When you're in a battle, the last thing you wanna do is praise God. You wanna rant and complain. But we must get out of our feelings and learn to lean into what we know about God. God inhabits the praises of his people. He is a present help in a time of trouble. He didn't bring us this far for us to fall on our faces now! We must come to ourselves like the Prodigal Son and not let what we see with our natural eyes make us doubt what is happening in the Spirit.

Anchor yourself in the Word, so when the winds and waves of life start knocking down everything around you, you can walk through the fire and not even smell like smoke. These storms, they be storming! And sometimes it gets so hard, we just wanna give up! But honey, you will get the victory if you faint not! Hallelujah!

It's all in our minds. It's with the mind we serve the Lord, so in these moments, you must learn to encourage yourself in the Lord. Satan does not want your car, he doesn't want your house, and he can't have your spirit if you already belong to God, so instead, he'll use those things that matter most to you to take your peace, to rob you of your joy. His # 1 goal is for you not to believe. He's super petty and very bitter! Just because he can't go back to heaven and have a relationship with God, through his son Jesus Christ, he wants to make sure we don't either. He is the original hater!

God would not give you the desire if it didn't serve a greater purpose. And he made you just like you are because you fit the description of your purpose. Right now, you already have inside you everything you need to be who God has purposed you to be. Everybody who left was supposed to leave because with them present, you would not finish the assignment.

Our character is developed when we are put in situations where our character is tested. God knew I would need patience for where he was taking me, so he gave me twins. In the everyday tasks of taking care of them, I developed patience. I didn't have patience before the twins! I became a more patient person. I wouldn't get so upset so quickly. I would lie one down and then put the other to sleep. As soon as both of them were down, I would sleep for 30 minutes before the first one was up, ready to start the cycle again. I didn't get mad, I just picked them up with love and started the process over. The moments when I was in a dark place were the moments I grew the fastest! He develops us and prepares us in the dark place to be ready for what is next. Don't get it twisted! The next is coming! If you're in a dark place right now, take a 30-second praise break because he is preparing you for what's next!

Sometimes you have to walk around your house telling yourself, "I am more than a conqueror in Christ Jesus." "I am confident that he who started a good work in me will perfect it until the day of Jesus Christ." Remind the devil that he has no real power! Remind the devil that no weapon formed against you shall be able to prosper. That a day is coming when Jesus is gonna throw him in a fiery pit for all eternity! It is why things are getting so crazy, the devil knows he is running out of time and he is the one freaking out! So encourage yourself in those seasons! Remember who you are in Christ when you wanna lie in bed and listen to old R&B songs all day and drink cheap wine.

Your desires change over time, and focusing on that one desire is not where it's at! As we continue to grow with Jesus, our desires grow. Naturally, we are only looking at what is in front of us. We are looking at one main goal. But we serve a God who is looking at how our movements will impact generations. He is Eternal, so our desire for 2025 has less to do with this year and more to do with our great-great-grandkids! He has a greater plan that must be revealed to us through his Holy Spirit. He changes our desires as we go deeper into Him. Think about it. The things you desire at 10 are not the same desires you had at 20, which are not the same at 30, 40, 50, 60, or even 70. And what's even more amazing is that the main thing you desire right now will change when you're 60 and change again when you're 70. One thing leads to the next thing. But the foundation of all your desires should be rooted in building a legacy that will last, and it can only last if it's built on the Kingdom. If you #SOK, Stand on Kingdom. The desires of your heart are a small piece of the bigger picture for your life. The desires are there to lead you into your calling. So the plan that God had in mind when he created you will come to pass by you trusting him through the steps.

After all I have done in my life, my only desire is to complete the mission God has created for me. It was what I was sent to do. So that when I am at the end of my life and getting ready to meet Jesus on Judgment Day, I know I'm going to heaven, not worried about that because I am saved, but I wanna make sure I fulfilled my purpose. That what he called me for, set me apart for before the foundation of the world, was accomplished. So have courage and go after your desires, it is your assignment for this season.

Examine your heart and ask yourself what are the things you desire for your family, your career, your health, and for yourself. Are those desires rooted in the Word of God? Then find a quiet place and talk with Jesus about what is in your heart. Ask him to give you the courage to accept his desires and watch God take you to places beyond your wildest imagination. My one desire to take care of kids took me from going back to school to now owning multiple businesses. My one desire to kick it with Jesus more led to me being a whole minister and soon-to-be pastor of a church. Me! Really, God, you play too much.

He gave me a desire to serve his people. The closer I got to him, the more he started rubbing off on me! I got more than I asked for because he put the desire in me, but I had to do the work! Listen, sha baby! I tell you. You got to birth that thing! It's so real! Work everyday, grinding, stretching, humbling yourself, and seeking his face. It's also some earthly work reaching laws and rules. Learning how to be a good communicator, a good leader, good with money, and learning how to manage your time. I had to forgive those who hurt me, and the betrayal was great! I had to get back to the church where I would grow with other Believers, and most importantly, I had to start being about God's business and trusting Him on some next-level stuff. I had to spend some real time alone with Him and His Word. Turning off my phone, sitting on my back porch, and sitting still in his presence with my thoughts engulfed in his unfailing love for me. There are no shortcuts; you have to have a real relationship with him, and you have to do the work. But when you know Him and He knows you, you will skip the line! The desires He gave you will change your life, change your community, and change a generation! Don't be afraid. Get on it like that, somebody gotta do it! In my Kendrick Lamar voice, smiling at that camera during the Super Bowl halftime show. Why not you?

Eyes have not seen, ears have not heard, nor has it entered into the hearts of man the things God has in plan for those who love him. In other words, God is about to blow your mind!

CHAPTER 8
You Can Be Whatever You Want to Be

By: Minister Herbert Poole

"I can do all things through Christ who strengthens me."
—Philippians 4:13 NKJV

This popular passage of Scripture is often referenced to support our own personal agendas and vain pursuits. Seldom having little, if anything, to do with pursuing or accomplishing what God has planned or desires for us.

At the time of writing this letter to the congregation of Believers in Philippi, the Apostle Paul is imprisoned in Rome. He is writing to encourage others while he is suffering persecution and hardship. He opens this letter by referring to himself as a slave of Christ Jesus. The purpose behind our motivation makes a world of difference.

How many of us have heard this at different points and times from various individuals? This affirmation is usually followed by one of these all-too-familiar phrases.

"If you just focus on your schoolwork."
"If you'd just apply yourself."
"If you get good enough grades."
"If you just connect to the right people."

"If you run in the right circles."
"If you'd just stop hanging around with those losers."
"If you play your cards right."
"If you put yourself first and stop trying to cater to everyone else."

And the list goes on. I'll suffice it to say you get the point.

Many of us, for one reason or another, struggle with confidence in believing that we can do, be, or accomplish something of significance in our lifetime. There is often some foothold our adversary has gained early in our lives that resonates in our hearts and minds. It holds us captive, similar to the chains and ropes used on a baby elephant to restrain it. As the elephant grows larger and stronger, even though the chains or ropes are no longer a match for its strength, it has long since given up the hope of freeing itself. But like the elephant, we too can break free.

These words of encouragement are offered to cheer us on to greatness. To encourage us to push beyond the limitations that we, ourselves, or society, have placed upon us. There is usually no malice or ill intent behind the voices of those who utter these words. The speaker conveying this message has our best interests at heart.

There is an old quote, often attributed to Albert Einstein. "Everybody is a genius. But if you judge a fish by its ability to climb a tree, it will live its whole life believing that it is stupid." While the origin of this quote remains a subject of debate, I believe we can glean something valuable from it.

We don't all possess the same gifts, talents, and abilities. But I believe we all have something of individual value and significance to offer. The key is discovering what our Creator had in mind when He meticulously designed and stitched us together. When He was carefully and purposefully planning and writing each letter, word, paragraph, and chapter of our lives.

> *"Before I formed you in the womb I knew you; Before you were born I sanctified you; I ordained you a prophet to the nations."*
> *—Jeremiah 1:5 NKJV*

God had a purpose and plan for your life before you were born. That concept can be difficult for many of us to fully comprehend. Especially because many of us may still be grappling with the question of who God is in the first place. In a culture where many are seeking to find and live their own "truth," it feels somewhat inhibiting, even controlling. After all, who wants to feel like they are not the master of their fate?

Let me be the first to say I don't have this whole freewill versus predestination thing all figured out. I wish I did. I do believe that God is omniscient and knows all things. Scripture lets us know in Romans 5:8 that while we were yet sinners, Jesus died for us. It tells us in Philippians 2:13 that it is God who works in us both to will and to do for His good pleasure.

Yet, we are instructed to present our bodies as a living sacrifice, holy and acceptable unto God. The Apostle Paul says to make our calling and election sure. To lay aside every weight and sin that would so easily distract us. He speaks in 1 Corinthians 9:27 about bringing his flesh under subjection, lest after preaching to others, he be a castaway. It is not the Father's will that any should perish. But Jesus tells us many will stand before Him testifying of works that they've done in His name, and sadly, He will tell them to depart from Him because He never knew them. What this says to me is that while we serve a sovereign God, we also have choices to make. We can choose to love and serve Him. Does this mean we'll walk the straight and narrow perfectly? Absolutely not! I believe Peter was a perfect example of this. One minute, he's sharing the revelation of who Christ is, and the next, he's trying to discourage Him from going to the cross. In case you're not familiar, this all happens within a matter of eight verses of Scripture in Matthew 16.

The primary calling and purpose that we all have is to reconcile with God. This means restoring our relationship with God, which was broken by sin.

And, as Scripture makes clear to us, that only comes through acceptance of Jesus' atoning work for us on the cross of Calvary. This is literally where the rubber meets the road. The true meaning of life starts here. It's kind of like that starting spot on most board games that you may have played.

Most of us don't receive a declaration as plain and clear as the prophet Jeremiah regarding God's calling upon our lives. But our purpose, simply put, is to bring glory to God! How we do that varies as much as each of us differs from the other. Who you are, your characteristics and traits, experiences, capabilities, capacity, knowledge, strengths, weaknesses, abilities, skills, convictions, revelations, insights, understanding, and, most importantly, your relationship with God.

GOD declared that Abraham would be a father of many nations before Isaac or Jacob were ever born. Isaiah prophesied about King Cyrus 200 years before he was born, saying that he would command the rebuilding of Jerusalem and the temple. An angel foretells Zechariah of the birth and mission of John the Baptist.

There are some aspirations that we can have in life that are within the realm of possibility. Although they may not conform to our Creator's plan and purpose for our lives, they are goals that we might pursue and attain, given the necessary course of action and opportunities. So, to say this statement is completely erroneous would be incorrect.

As I ponder certain situations that might be considered roadblocks or hindrances to individuals pursuing various roles, professions, or identities, I must also acknowledge many of the advances in modern medicine and technology. There are things that, at one time or another, were deemed beyond the scope of reason or possibility. But they are now considered viable options.

Someone who is blind becoming an airplane pilot or limousine chauffeur. An individual who cannot taste anything becoming a world-famous food critic. A person becoming a dog, horse, bird, or fish. A black person becoming white or vice versa.

Don't get me wrong, I believe without a doubt that God still performs miracles! I know that technology is still moving forward. However, at this stage of our evolution, there are just some things that would still be classified as highly unlikely to happen or impossible.

There are aspirations in life that we can achieve, which are simply outside of the will of God for our lives. Some of them could be considered good or honorable. While others would be deemed deplorable or a menace to society.

The following quote is from the 1981 movie, "Chariots of Fire":

> *"I believe God made me for a purpose,*
> *but He also made me fast.*
> *And when I run, I feel His pleasure."*
> –Eric Liddell

Some questions to ponder:

- Am I bringing God pleasure and delight?
- Does what I am planning and striving to become glorify God in some way?
- Is this God's highest and best purpose for my life?
- What education, training, or mentoring do I need to further develop the gift, talent, and ability God has entrusted to me?
- Am I allowing the things the world uses to measure success to guide my path?
- Will what I desire to become draw me closer to God or pull me further away from Him?

CHAPTER 9
Communion is Just a Tradition

By: Minister Jacquelyn Jones

There is a sacred invitation extended to every soul, an invitation to a table prepared by the hands of a loving God. At this table, the bread is more than bread, and the wine is more than wine; they are the doorway into something much more profound: a transformative communion with the Living God.

Many of us have carried unanswered questions, things we sensed but never fully understood, things we were never taught to ask, or were told not to question God, leaving us to live with brain fog, spiritual dullness, or weariness, wondering if God still sees, hears, or moves.

This journey you are about to embark on is an uncovering, a reawakening, using bread and wine as an example in place of God's body and blood.

Communion is the ice breaker—the gateway to a greater conversation - clearing confusion, calling us to restoration, and drawing us back into fellowship with Him.

God is still alive. He still sees, and He still hears every thought. He desires that we ask, seek, knock, and find Him. He longs for us to be saved, healed, and delivered to all the Jews and the Gentiles alike, for He cares for all humanity. As you walk through these pages, may your heart be stirred to return to the table, and may you discover the wholeness God intended for you.

Communion is More Than Bread and Wine

For many, communion is a familiar practice; it is an integral part of church life that we partake in regularly. But have you ever stopped to wonder what it truly represents and why it holds such significance in our faith? What if we approached it with a deeper understanding of its transformative power and the intimate connection it offers with Christ?

Why do we take communion? We all have our own personal relationship with God and have a responsibility to understand why we are taking communion. Romans 14:12 (KJV) states, "So then each of us will give an account of himself to God." For some, it may feel like just another ritual. Simply taking a piece of bread and a sip of wine (or juice) is still a symbol of Christ's sacrifice. But is there more to it than just the physical act? What deeper meaning lies within this sacred practice?

As we explore communion through research and the Bible, I'm reminded of how old school preachers would begin in a dramatic fashion, "And the Bible said…" Then, continue explaining that communion goes much deeper than a mere act of remembering; it is a sacrificial moment meant to connect us deeply with Christ's death, His resurrection, and the covenant that He established with His people.

Uncovering Misunderstanding About Communion

Now, let's look at misunderstandings surrounding communion and challenge some of these commonly held beliefs. We will consider how these beliefs are passed down through generations and highlight the profound sacredness and significance of this practice. Some of these beliefs are rooted in truth; others are longstanding misunderstandings that need to be addressed whether you are new to the faith or have participated in communion for years. To truly experience the richness of this sacrament, we must gently examine and release what no longer aligns with Scripture and Spirit.

The Lord's Supper is not just about the ritual. It's an opportunity to renew our covenant with God by honoring Christ's sacrifice, and to participate in a spiritual act of unity with Him and His Church. As we delve into this exploration of communion's deeper meaning, let's open our hearts to what God has revealed through this sacred sacrament and understand why it's essential for our spiritual growth and connection to Christ.

Many people approach communion as just a routine part of church life, something we do because it's expected or because it's part of the tradition. However, it's important to recognize that communion holds profound spiritual significance. It is not just a ritual; it is a sacrament that connects us with the very heart of our faith.

Some view it as a passive observance, a simple act of eating bread and drinking wine during service, but that perspective is a misinterpretations of what is really being presented. However, approaching communion with such a limited perspective means missing out on its true power. The bread symbolizes the Body of Christ, broken for us; the wine represents His blood, poured out for the forgiveness of sins. This sacred moment calls us to reflect deeply on Jesus' sacrifice and the redemption it offers.

Another misunderstanding that needs dispelling is the idea that communion is only for the "worthy." This can create unnecessary barriers, causing people to shy away from participating because they feel unworthy or disconnected from the church. The truth is, communion is not about perfection; it's about coming together as a community, acknowledging our need for grace, and remembering Christ's invitation to us all.

For a deeper experience of communion, we must first dispel these myths and approach the sacrament with open hearts and minds. By understanding its true meaning, we invite transformation into our lives. Communion is an opportunity for spiritual renewal, a chance to draw nearer to God, and a way to unite with our fellow Believers in a shared expression of faith.

Let us strive to approach communion not as a ritual to be checked off but as a sacred encounter with the divine, where we reflect on Christ's love and sacrifice, embrace His grace, and strengthen our connection to one another.

Have you ever wondered why we take communion? Let's take a moment to go deeper and explore its true significance.

Breaking The Myths:

Myth #1 Communion is Just a Tradition

- As previously mentioned, communion is not just a religious ritual. It is a sacred act of remembrance, a way to honor Christ's sacrifice and the New Covenant. It's not merely a symbolic gesture but a practice that connects Believers to the very presence of Christ.
- Scripture: Luke 22:19-20 says This is my body, which is given for you: this do in remembrance of me. Likewise also the cup, This cup is the New Testament in my blood, which is shaded for you.

Myth #2 It's Only for the Worthy

- This myth can discourage people who feel unworthy. However, communion is for those who recognize their need for Christ and accept His invitation to partake, even in their imperfection.
- Scripture: 1 Corinthians 11:28 says, "But Let a man examine himself, and so let him eat of the bread, and drink of that cup."

Myth # 3 It's Only a Memorial

- Communion is more than remembering; it's about participation in the covenant and a declaration of Christ's death until He returns. It's an act of spiritual unity and intimacy with Christ.
- Scripture: 1 Corinthians 10:16-17 "The cup of blessing that we bless, is it not a participation in the blood of Christ? The bread that we break, is it not a partition in the Body of Christ?"

Myth #4 Communion is Only for Church Members and You Must Be in Good Standing

- The truth is, communion isn't owned by Catholicism, Baptist, Pentecostal, or any denomination. It belongs to Christ and His Church.

Myth 5: You Can Only Take Communion in a Church Setting

- The early church broke bread in their homes. You can communion with God anywhere. (1 Corinthians 11:25-26 NKJV)

Theological Reflection: Communion as a Means of Grace

- Theologically, communion is a means of grace and a channel through which Believers draw near to God. It is a time when we receive spiritual nourishment, not just through the physical elements, but through the Holy Spirit, who works in and through us during this act of faith. It is a holy moment of renewal, an invitation to experience a deeper intimacy with Christ. As we partake in this communion, we open our hearts to the transformative power of His grace, strengthening our relationship with Him and one another.

We focus our Scriptures here:

> **John 6:51,** "I am the living bread that came down from heaven. If anyone eats this bread, he will live forever."
> **Matthew 26:29,** "But I say unto you, I will not drink again of this fruit of the vine until that day when I drink it again with you in my Father's Kingdom."

The Importance of Understanding Communion:

This chapter focuses on the importance of understanding communion, based on the principle from **Proverbs 4:7** ("In all thy getting, get understanding"). The meaning behind communion is to avoid merely going through the motions.

1. **The Need for Understanding:**
    - Why understanding communion is crucial. Many misunderstandings arise because people don't fully grasp the spiritual significance of this sacrament. As Proverbs 4:7 states, wisdom and understanding are essential to living a fulfilling Christian life, and that includes understanding the sacraments.
    - A Call to Reflect: The understanding of communion invites a deeper encounter with Christ, moving us beyond habit into meaningful worship and transformation.
2. **Invitation to Reflect Deeper:**
    - *If communion is a time of spiritual renewal and participation in Christ's life, how can it transform your walk with Him?"*
    - It invites you, the readers, to reflect on a deeper purpose of communion, which goes beyond tradition or habit. It's about a heartfelt connection to Jesus. Let me encourage you to see communion as an opportunity to renew your covenant with God and commit to living in the fullness of His grace.
3. **Scriptural Foundation:**
    - 1 Corinthians 11:26: *"For as often as you eat this bread and drink the cup, you proclaim the Lord's death until he comes."*

- John 6:53-56: *"Unless you eat the flesh of the Son of Man and drink His blood, you have no life in you... Whoever feeds on My flesh and drinks My blood has eternal life."*

4. **The Significance of Communion Today:**
   - How communion has practical significance today. It's an opportunity for spiritual reflection and self-examination (1 Corinthians 11:28). It is a moment to realign our lives with Christ and to celebrate his victory over sin and death.
   - Theological reflection: Understanding communion as a sacrament invites Believers into deeper fellowship with Christ. It is a grace-filled moment to renew the Christian's spiritual journey.
5. **Reflection:**
   - Learn to reevaluate yourself by asking yourself if you truly understand why you are taking communion.
   - Is it just a tradition that we do because our mama did it or grandparents did it, or is it a powerful act that symbolizes their connection with Christ's sacrifice?

From Genesis to Revelation

1. **Genesis**: Created for Communion
   - God walked with Adam and Eve (Genesis 3:8).
   - Sin broke fellowship, but God promised a Redeemer (Genesis 3:15).
2. **The Eyes Were Opened**: Awareness of Separation
   - Adam and Eve's eyes were opened to their nakedness and shame (Genesis 3:7).

- Similarly, many today live unaware of their need for God until He opens their spiritual eyes.
- I used to think like you ("There was a time I took communion lightly... but God...")

When it Became Real to Me:

For years, I sat in church and took communion without really thinking about it. It was just another part of the service, something we did. I was just going through the motions like everyone else on my row. I didn't feel bad, scared, or confused. I listened to what was being said, and I just took communion. I thought I was just fine because I didn't do anything wrong.

But God, in His mercy, opened my eyes. He showed me that communion isn't just about a ritual; it's about relationships. Through my personal study, praying and fasting, and moments of quiet conviction, God helped me to hear His voice above the noise and the smoke of this world.

He invited me to *seek* Him and learn of his statutes according to Jeremiah 29:13, and to experience the sacredness of communion as a moment of encounter. I realized that from the Garden to the Cross, and from the Cross to the coming Kingdom, He's been calling us back to Himself.

1. **The Two Adams**:
   - First Adam brought death through sin; Jesus (the Second Adam) brought life through obedience (1 Corinthians 15:45, Romans 5:17–19).
   - Communion celebrates the victory of the Second Adam!

2. **The Invitation Continues**:
    - Old Testament sacrifices pointed forward to Jesus.
    - Jesus fulfilled the promise at the Last Supper.
3. **Revelation**: Communion Fulfilled Forever
    - The Marriage Supper of the Lamb (Revelation 19:6-9).
    - Jesus promised, "I will not drink again of the fruit of the vine until the Kingdom of God comes" (Luke 22:18).
    - In heaven, we will feast with Him again at His table, *forever united.*
4. **Closing Invitation**:
    - Communion is a preview of the feast to come.
    - God's call is still going out: "Come to the table."

An Invitation to Restoration

The Eucharist or Holy Communion is not just a ceremony; it is a call back to the heart of God. It is an invitation to restoration, forgiveness, and a deeper fellowship with Him.

Every time we partake, we remember that we were bought with a price, that the broken body and shed blood of Jesus made a way for every barrier between God and man to be torn down.

God is not distant. He is closer than our very breath, waiting for us to simply ask, seek, and surrender. Whether you are Jew or Gentile, young or old, near or far, he cares for you.

This invitation is for all who hunger and thirst for righteousness, all who are tired of living separated from the fullness of life He offers.

The Bread of Life has been broken for you. The cup of salvation has been poured out.

Will you come? Will you take your seat at the table?

In conclusion, remember that the Christian faith is an ongoing journey of growth and deepening understanding. As you approach communion, I encourage you to continue asking questions and seeking a deeper intimacy with Christ. Let each moment at the Lord's table be an opportunity to see with fresh eyes and a heart full of reverence, drawing closer to Him in ways that transform your life.

Just know it's never too late, come while there is still time.

There is still room at the cross for you.

Stay Tuned: God has given me a vision to create a Podcast on communion.

I'm launching a new podcast that invites you on a journey *from Genesis to Revelation* to rediscover the powerful, sacred meaning of communion.

CHAPTER 10
The Power of His Might

By: Minister Ron Campbell

A Breakdown of Philippians 4:12-13

Understanding Strength and Contentment in Faith

Philippians 4:12-13 is a powerful passage from the New Testament, written by the Apostle Paul to the church in Philippi. These verses hold deep meaning and offer profound insights into Christian faith, contentment, and reliance on God's strength. The verses read as follows:

"I know what it is to be in need, and I know what it is to have plenty. I have learned the secret of being content in any and every situation, whether well fed or hungry, whether living in plenty or in want. I can do all this through him who gives me strength."

Context of the Passage

To fully grasp the significance of Philippians 4:12-13, it is essential to understand the broader context of the passage. Paul wrote this letter during his imprisonment, likely in Rome, between AD 60 and 62. Despite his circumstances, Paul exudes joy, gratitude, and encouragement throughout the letter. His message to the Philippians centers on living a life worthy of the gospel, finding joy in Christ, and being unified in purpose and love.

Paul's Experiences

Paul begins verse 12 by reflecting on his varied experiences: "I know what it is to be in need, and I know what it is to have plenty." This statement highlights Paul's diverse life experiences, which included both times of abundance and times of severe hardship. As a missionary, Paul faced numerous trials, including imprisonment, beatings, shipwrecks, and periods of hunger and destitution. Yet, he also experienced significant moments of support, generosity, and provision from fellow Believers and the communities he served, underscoring the positive encounters he had during his journey and the role of community in his ministry.

The Secret of Contentment

Paul goes on to say, "I have learned the secret of being content in any and every situation, whether well fed or hungry, whether living in plenty or in want." Here, Paul reveals a valuable lesson he has learned through his experiences: the secret of contentment. Contentment, in this context, is not merely a passive acceptance of circumstances but an active trust in God's provision and sovereignty. It is a state of inner peace and satisfaction that we can diligently cultivate, and it transcends external conditions.

The Source of Strength

In verse 13, Paul declares, "I can do all this through him who gives me strength." This well-known verse is often cited as a source of encouragement and motivation. However, it is crucial to understand its meaning within the context of contentment. Paul's ability to endure and thrive in various circumstances is not due to his strength or resilience but is rooted in his dependence on Christ. The "him" in this verse refers to Jesus Christ, who empowers Paul to face any situation with grace and confidence.

Misinterpretations and Clarifications

Philippians 4:13 can be misinterpreted as a blanket promise for success in all endeavors. However, its primary focus is on the strength to endure and remain content regardless of life's challenges. Paul's message emphasizes that true strength and contentment come from a relationship with Christ, not from self-reliance or worldly achievements.

Lessons for Believers

The lessons from Philippians 4:12-13 are timeless and applicable to Believers today. Here are some key takeaways:

- Embrace Contentment: Like Paul, Believers are called to find contentment in all circumstances. This requires a shift in perspective, focusing on God's faithfulness rather than external conditions.
- Depend on Christ: True strength comes from a relationship with Christ. Believers are encouraged to rely on Jesus for strength, guidance, and support in every situation.

- Trust in God's Provision: Paul's experiences remind Believers that God is sovereign and provides for His children. Trusting in God's provision allows Believers to face uncertainties with confidence and peace.

Application in Daily Life

Applying the principles of Philippians 4:12-13 in daily life involves practical steps and a mindset rooted in faith. Here are some ways to incorporate these lessons:

Practice Gratitude

Gratitude is a powerful tool for cultivating contentment, according to 1 Timothy 6:6. By regularly acknowledging and giving thanks for God's blessings, Believers can shift their focus from what they lack to what they have. This practice helps to develop a heart of contentment and trust in God's provision.

Lean on Scripture and Prayer

Studying the Bible and maintaining a consistent prayer life is essential for spiritual growth and reliance on Christ. Through Scripture, Believers can find encouragement, wisdom, and strength. Prayer allows Believers to communicate with God, express their needs, and seek His guidance and support.

Seek Community and Support

Paul's relationship with the Philippians exemplifies the importance of community and mutual support. Believers are encouraged to build strong relationships with fellow Christians, offering and receiving support, encouragement, and accountability. Being part of a faith community provides a network of support that strengthens one's walk with Christ.

Focus on Eternal Perspective

Paul's contentment was deeply rooted in his eternal perspective. By focusing on God's promises and the hope of eternal life, Believers can navigate temporal challenges with a sense of peace and purpose. This eternal perspective helps to alleviate anxiety and fosters a resilient faith.

Conclusion

Philippians 4:12-13 offers profound insights into the nature of true contentment and strength. Paul's words remind Believers that contentment is not dependent on external circumstances but is found in a deep, abiding relationship with Christ. By relying on Jesus for strength and trusting in God's provision, Believers can face any situation with confidence and peace of mind. Embracing these principles in daily life leads to a more resilient, joyful, and faith-filled existence.

As Believers meditate on these verses and apply their lessons, they are invited to experience the transformative power of contentment and strength that comes from a life rooted in Christ. Through gratitude, Scripture, prayer, community, and an eternal perspective, Believers can navigate life's complexities with unwavering faith and unshakeable contentment.

Personal Testimony

"I can do all things through Christ, which strengthens me," is what we learned from Grandma and Grandpa back in the old days. We really didn't know anything else other than what we heard from them. Was it the right thing or not? The manifestation of the things that God has for us comes at a time when we realize what He is trying to teach us, and not a minute before. It takes years to understand what God is saying to us before we begin to even get close to getting it right. We are spiritual beings having a human experience, after all, and we all fall short of His glory regardless of background, geographical location, or complexity.

A Mississippian was reported whipped with a piece of cable for trying to register for the primary in 1946. A shoe repairman and a taxi driver admitted to being paid **$25** to warn off black people from the polls. In the meantime, even though this happened, the Evers brothers still officially became so-called "Agitators."

Their efforts caught the attention of the NAACP and Dr. Theodore Rosevelt Mason Howard, proving that if you keep walking the path that God has for you, it will come to pass. My father was a man of little words, but after all he had observed growing up, he had gained a knowledge unsurpassable in his memory banks. I don't know much other than what he told me about his childhood, but just like the Evers family, he had trials and tribulations back in those times.

Peter responds in Matthew 14:28 (NIV) saying, "...Lord, if it's you, tell me to come to you on water." If we really look back at what they endured, Jesus called them out of the boat to walk by faith and not by sight. John 15:4 KJV tells us, "Abide in me, and I in you. As the branch cannot bear fruit of itself, except it abide in the vine, no more can ye, except ye abide in me." Isa 40:31 NLT reads, "But those who trust in the Lord will find new strength. They will soar high on wings like eagles. They will run and not grow weary. They will walk and not faint."

It took all of me to make it from the 70s until now due to the many changes of the times. Being born into an era that was coming out of, or shall I say, being birthed into a season of unrest because it was just a changing of the guard. If you are familiar with security, you don't get much rest. Jimmy Carter would soon be president, and the lifestyle change would be helpful to all in this era. The 70s still had its problems just as present times, yet we still move forward because the work is never complete. Just as Jesus died for our sins, we must glorify Him in every way possible.

I had a good friend in fifth grade in Houston, Texas, whom I will not, for the sake of the family, say his name. We had a friendship like no one else. We enjoyed the same hobbies and had a lot in common in the way we thought. I had friends in my neighborhood, but this friend was like a brother in the way that we hung out at school together when no one else would hang out with us; maybe we just didn't fit in with the others in those ways, but still, we played and socialized with them. Country boy he was, and my mind was country and city all at the same time. Even though I hadn't done most of the things he had done, my family had come from the lifestyle that he was used to having. It's ironic for two people to have the same mindset but have not had the same experiences, and connect on those levels.

The school year was ending, and we all talked about what the summer would bring. Some of my friends had big plans with their grandparents, while some had only minimal thoughts of what the summer could bring. My summers were usually spent with my grandparents, only a few miles away from my home. I had a whole set of other friends in my grandparents' community. They had different temperaments and different ways of doing things.

A normal day would consist of us playing baseball, football, and basketball. On other days, we scheduled for 2-day events as if we were pros, and our games usually followed a baseball or football game that aired on TV.

This reminds me of the ministerial class that I attended at PHSOM (The Potter's House School of Ministry), in the aspect of being tested after every chapter or book of the Bible that was introduced. The instructor would explain each chapter of the Bible, encouraging us to research commentaries, explore definitions in text, and take a deeper look at the people of the Bible. Every teacher had his or her own personality and style, which reminds me of John 15:2 (KJV). It reads, "Every branch in me that beareth not fruit he taketh away: and every branch that beareth fruit, he purgeth it, that it may bring forth more fruit." This is a text that reflects on what it is to be a student, and the roots of the instructor teaching the lesson. If the instructor's roots run deep and or entangled with the leader of the garden, then the fruit that is beareth, he will purgeth it that it may bring more fruit.

The summer had passed, and it was once time to go back to school again, not that it was a bad thing, but time goes by fast. It was an exciting time because we got to show off the new kicks and Levi's, and Polo or OP shirts. Oh, and don't forget the boots. You see, I'm from Texas, where we sported Western wear also, snakeskin, turtle skin, ostrich, and so on. My brother wore boots all the time, so I was looking for the brother with the Wranglers and cowboy boots with a Polo on, but I couldn't find him, so I asked a mutual friend, and I couldn't believe the next thing he told me was true. My brother had passed trying to save his own relative from drowning; this was devastating to me because I saw him as a real brother, and that's how I remember him simply: my brother R.I.H. FH, we love you, Bruh. Christ strengthens us in ways we can't explain. Even as Believers in the faith, He amazes us with His grace and mercy. I still remember the people who shaped life and were a part of the everyday grind of life in those times. Paul expresses his confidence that God will help him endure anything and teaches Christians the ability to endure hardship and persecution, and whatever a person's circumstances, they can be content if they follow. Often, the verse is misused as a mystical incantation to defeat an enemy or complete a difficult task. This may be due to forming the thought that whatever evil done by the enemy comes your way, Jesus will help you defeat it. God doesn't step in all the time when the enemy is attacking you; rather, He has already given you the power to defeat the works of the enemy. Sometimes, it's not the enemy that's attacking you, it's God trying to let you know it's time to move forward.

Philippians 4

Exhortations to Stand Firm and Rejoice

The chapter begins with Paul urging the Philippians to stand firm in the Lord:

- Verse 1: "Therefore, my brothers and sisters, you whom I love and long for, my joy and crown, stand firm in the Lord in this way, dear friends!" Paul expresses his deep affection for the Philippians and encourages them to remain steadfast in their faith.
- Verses 2-3: Paul addresses a dispute between two women, Euodia and Syntyche, urging them to reconcile. He also asks a loyal companion to assist these women, recognizing their valuable contributions to the gospel.
- Verse 4: "Rejoice in the Lord always. I will say it again: Rejoice!" Paul emphasizes the importance of joy in the Christian life, regardless of circumstances.
- Verses 5-7: Paul advises the Philippians to be gentle and not to be anxious about anything. Instead, they should present their requests to God through prayer and thanksgiving, resulting in the peace of God guarding their hearts and minds.

Be anxious about nothing, Philippians 4:6. The Yiddish have a word (*Al tid'ag*) which means "do not worry." In the Sermon at the Mount, Jesus said, Don't worry about tomorrow, what you will drink, what you will eat, what you will wear. He told us to consider how the birds do not plant their crops and reap the harvest to store in their barns. "Your Father feeds them." You who are worried about your clothes consider the lilies of the field, they do not toil and spin, as referred to their spinning their yarn to make the material for the clothes.

Matthew 5:3-12

> *"Blessed are the poor in spirit, for theirs is the kingdom of heaven.*
> *Blessed are those who mourn, for they shall be comforted.*
> *Blessed are the meek, for they shall inherit the earth.*
> *Blessed are those who hunger and thirst for righteousness, for they shall be satisfied.*
> *Blessed are the merciful, for they shall receive mercy.*
> *Blessed are the pure in heart, for they shall see God.*
> *Blessed are the peacemakers, for they shall be called sons of God.*
> *Blessed are those who are persecuted for righteousness' sake, for theirs is the kingdom of heaven.*
> *Blessed are you when others revile you and persecute you and utter all kinds of evil against you falsely on my account.*
> *Rejoice and be glad, for your reward is great in heaven, for so they persecuted the prophets who were before you."*

Matthew 5 connects with Philippians 4:13 in that we are blessed in the ways that Jesus stated, and if we are blessed in those ways, then surely, we can do all things through him who strengthens us. Today, we have a new era of people who may not understand the upbringing of the people before them, their fathers and grandfathers, mothers and grandmothers, greats, and great-greats. This disconnect needs to be repaired because we, as people, may be lost and not realize that we can do things with the full knowledge that we have today. Whatever good work you do, do it because it's the right thing to do. Do it because it's necessary. Do it to make change for the better;

don't do it for credit. The power of His might is more than enough to carry forward your good intentions of the heart that He already knows.

A Western shirt with a low haircut and a missing tooth in the front is the setting of a childhood picture of me, taken in elementary school. I was excited to go to school before I even started, always asking my mother when I would start school, and she said I would start school when I was five years old. Mama had books on a bookshelf in the living room area in a nook where we had the component set and albums. The component set, for those that are wondering, was a stereo set with speakers that were wired together with plug-ins. Albums and 45s played on the top, and the radio was on the bottom with an equalizer. Parliament – Funkadelic, Blonde, The O'Jays, Maze and Frankie B are some of the artists from those times. The high school band playing nearby echoes all over the community as if they were in your backyard. The sound of music being played in the cars driving by, with Rockford Fosgate woofers humming in the neighborhood a mile away, kind of blended with the band's practice sessions. Getting ready to get out for the weekend, the music started getting louder as one of my friends crept down my dead-end street. Bright sun, the smell of freshly cut grass, and a hint of fabric softener from the clothing line behind the house filled the air as I walked out to get in the car with my Bruhs.

Everything was done before leaving home, as it should have been, because this was life in those times. Mama said to do your chores before going anyplace, and that's what she meant; it wasn't a game or a joke. You either do it or stay at home, and I'm not one to stay in one spot, so work got done early most of the time, and sometimes, days before the weekend. Got to do what you got to do.

This brings back a lot of memories, and I can almost reach out and touch the knob on the back door of my childhood home and turn it, pushing it open to see my mom in the kitchen cooking dinner or doing some other chores. Twelve midnight on a Saturday night, stepping in like we used to do (no need to explain, we've all been there at one time). Dad may step out of his bedroom and say, "Where have you been? It's late." Ok, so we won't go into all the details on this round. I'm in a place where writing this chapter of my life has a lot of history and literature all around. Some old, some newer, and some current. Woolworths Diner only changed so much from the sixties to the seventies. I was barely able to sit at the counter. Black Flags, Blue Waters, Life on the Mississippi, the Constitution of the United States, Nixonland, some things that I see, Battle Briefings, Lincoln vs Davis, oh Douglass, John Lewis's Carry on. God made us in His image, and we are still trying to figure it out today in 2025.

When will we realize that His hand is at the wheel and we are the passengers in this thing called life, for we are experiencing a life of flesh, and it will not last? I have met many people from different walks of life in my time on this earth, and I have learned a lot from those that I crossed paths with. We come with varying mindsets, so be prepared to be tested in every kind of way, but have an open mind about what you are learning. Life can change in an instant, and we can regret not doing something that we should have done after these changes. Be the first in your family to do something about positively changing your family's circumstances and breaking the chains that hold your family's future back.

At fourteen, fifteen, and seventeen years old, Mom and Dad were in and out of the hospital, and things started looking bad from my side of the retina. I'm seeing Mom at the hospital with Dad, and Dad at the hospital with Mom, and life is different at this point. It was rough at times holding down the dishwashing and laundry while Mom was in the hospital. Getting yourself ready for school in the mornings and not hearing her voice was different and strange all at the same time, but you push on, and, in the end, God works it all out. After all, she prepared you for this in the beginning with the yard work, washing clothes, cleaning the house, etc.

Political Insight

The changing of the guard in Washington has been a task in this term. It is testing the faith of every one of us, and those in the White House, yet we still rise to the occasion. What ifs and maybe we can't or yes, we can echo throughout the atmosphere. We go high when they go low is the theme. What about God being the greatest of all is the question I have for you, and His mercy enduring forever being the highlight of the century. After all, did He or did He not create every living thing? Ok, I think you should know this part. My point is, man has actually forgotten his heavenly Father, the Creator of all creations, and has placed himself on high.

My stance in life couldn't afford college, so please excuse me if my grammar is different from yours. God said, Go forth into all the world and preach the gospel. This old, wretched man that I am can do right and will do the work of the Lord.

God moves in directions that we do not understand. Even when we aren't aware of what He is doing, He is moving in silence. We can do all things because He is all things, and all things He is. He has granted gifts to all of us, and the gifts He has granted are everlasting and abundant. We as men try to put on a façade that we are so masculine and overwhelmingly strong to the point that we hinder ourselves from life as God intended. "Performative masculinity, the intentional display of traditionally masculine traits and behaviors to conform to societal expectations and prove one's masculinity, for the purpose of validation." (Liu et al., 2022, p. n.p.)[15]

It seems we have missed the mark on being a man of humbleness and subtleness to our families and friends, as if we will be judged to the firmament of hell in the minds of men. We have lost the ties between big brother and little brother; each one teaches one for more money and more limelight.

Genesis 1:1 ASV reads, "In the beginning, God created the heavens and the earth." And picks up in Genesis 2 verses 5 and 7 ASV, "When the Lord God made the earth and the heavens, neither wild plants nor grains were growing on the earth. Then, after some time of creating, God said let us make man in our image after our likeness." Now let's go back to Genesis 1:26 ASV where it reads, "…and let them have dominion over the fish of the sea, and over the fowl of the air, and over the cattle, and over every creeping thing that creepeth upon the earth."

Man has been given dominion over everything on the planet that God created, and now he has forgotten his Father, as if man himself was created by his own hand. I understand this very much because Abram brought a lot for us to deal with.

---

15 Liu, et al., (2022). Performative masculinity: A meta-ethnography of experiences of men in academic and clinical nursing. International Journal of Environmental Research and Public Health, 19, 14813. https://pmc.ncbi.nlm.nih.gov/articles/PMC9690486/

If we go on the journey to the place between Bethel and AI and call on the name of the Lord, we just may be able to rebuild this altar. Lot's flocks and herds and tents could not be supported by the land at that time, along with Abram's, so they couldn't dwell together. Maybe we have a "Lot" to part ways with before we can move forward. I'm just telling you what Genesis said; it's what we know, not what we heard. Sarah is my sister, but she is also my wife. No, I didn't marry my blood sister, but we have the same father. After all, Father did create them. Abraham denounced the fact that his alleged sister was his wife, but in 2025, that dog don't hunt. Excuse the slogan. So, the evening and the morning were the fourth day. Then, God said, let the waters abound with an abundance of living creatures, let birds fly above the earth across the face of the firmament of the heavens. Can we do the things that God has given us the power to do, or will we give the power back and forfeit our seat and crown? I can do all things through Christ because of the power of His might.

CHAPTER 11

Toughest Battles Goes to Strongest Soldiers

By: Minister Priscilla Jones

God gives His toughest battles to His strongest soldiers. What does that even mean? Let's take a look at the beginning.

The Bible says in John 1:1-4 (NIV): "In the beginning was the Word, and the Word was with God, and the Word was God. The same was in the beginning with God. All things were made by Him; and without Him was not anything made that was made. In Him was life; and the life was the light of men."

Before the fall of man, we had an open relationship with God. Adam knew God's voice, and because Adam was a good sheep, there was nothing Adam did that God didn't know about. He created him. Everything God made was very good. Even after Adam ate the forbidden fruit, God was still with him and Eve, but the sound was different. It would be equivalent to someone getting a hearing aid for the first time. The sound must be adjusted to match the rhythm and frequency of the ear. It takes a minute for it to be adjusted, and the person becomes accustomed to something they have always felt but could not hear.

The same happened with Adam and Eve. The world they were accustomed to had changed, but God didn't.

Now, if God stayed with them despite their new knowledge of good and evil, what makes us different? God's love never changed. It is still covered. Today, when we look at the adversities, hardships, and ordeals we face, God is still with us. When people post, chat, and talk about the things they are facing, someone immediately says, "God always gives His toughest battles to His strongest soldiers."

Where did this thought originate? Why are we taking motivational speeches and trying to turn them into Scriptures? God never said anything about giving out the "toughest battle" award.

His Word says in 1 Peter 5:7-8 (KJV), *"Casting all your care upon Him; for He careth for you. Be sober, be vigilant; because your adversary the devil, as a roaring lion, walketh about, seeking whom he may devour."*

I have watched as so many people have faced some of the worst, unimaginable situations in their lives. The scans came back with a diagnosis of cancer. The unexplainable emotions, thoughts, and worries. Receiving the call that a loved one didn't make it. The mother and father, whose child is having a difficult time in school, then receive the quote that it's going to cost an astronomical amount to fix the car.

On top of that, they have a major water leak in the home. They're already wondering, "Where is the very presence of God in all of this?" They are praying and believing, but something else happens, and the sound of their cry is different. Not realizing that God is still with them and covering them. Then someone walks up to them and says, "Ah, man, I'm sorry.

You know God always gives His toughest battles to His strongest soldiers."

Now, imagine being the woman who has been bleeding for twelve long years. She's already weak and

tired because she's bleeding, but she's still in the fight. She's losing energy and probably hopes that her life will change. She's probably heard that over and over again, "You'll never be healed," repeatedly. "Eww, she ain't dead yet."

After a while, it gets to be a cliché: I must be going through this because I'm the strongest soldier. Now, when times get hard, we're quoting Facebook motivational posts instead of the Word.

The Bible says in Matthew 24:35 (KJV),

> *"Heaven and earth shall pass away, but My words shall not pass away."*

So, she pressed through the stench of her odor, the shame she had to feel from the stares. *What can He offer you? You've already tried every physician in town, and no one can help you. What makes you think He has something to offer you?* Bleeding but determined, she pressed her way through. Thinking, *If I can just get to Jesus.* She gathered her last bit of strength and touched the borders of His garment. Immediately, the Bible says her blood stanched. When Jesus felt the virtue leave His body, He didn't turn and say to this woman, "Ah, there she is. One of my toughest soldiers." Ha! Imagine how she would have felt to hear Him speak these words. She probably would have used words that wouldn't have come from the King James Bible. The shame she already felt and had to endure to get here. The whispers that were felt out loud. The stares from those who thought, *You don't belong here.*

We've all had different experiences and have felt pain. We've been in situations for so long that we don't know what to do. Just as the woman with the issue of blood, we must continually reach out to God. We have to go back to communicating with God. Our situations make God seem so far away to the point we feel as though He doesn't care. That's not the case.

Hebrews 4:15-16 (KJV) states,

> *"For we have not an high priest which cannot be touched with the feeling of our infirmities; but was in all points tempted like as we are, yet without sin. Let us therefore come boldly unto the throne of grace, that we may obtain mercy, and find grace to help in time of need."*

Instead, we've introduced a curse into our bloodlines because, instead of speaking the Word over our situation, we go with whatever cultural ethos and TikTok theologians say. Now, when battles come, instead of casting all our worries on Him, we feel like we are in a *No Limit Soldier* boot camp. We replay in our minds that God gives His toughest battles to His strongest soldiers. That's not scriptural. The Word works if you use it.

Revelation 12:11 talks about us overcoming the enemy by the blood of the Lamb and the word of our testimonies. The church and the world are all mixed together. We have a generation of children lost, crying out to a God they don't believe is real. We have a desperation of people hungry for the Word, determined not to allow history to repeat itself.

Just like Adam and Eve, we know right from wrong, but the flesh rises. It's hard to pray at times because it's like, "God, you already know what I'm going through. This didn't catch You by surprise. Why me? Why does it feel like I'm always going through something? Are You even real? So-and-so always gets the latest of everything and posts about all their success. Why do I keep experiencing such hardships?"

We get frustrated with God because He gave us instructions, but we want to do things our way. Proverbs 3 instructs us to acknowledge God in all our ways, and He will direct our paths. It doesn't mean things will be easy, but just like with Adam and Eve and the woman with the issue of blood, God was with them. He's with us as well.

I remember Bishop T.D. Jakes preaching about the threshing floor. He said, "Your experience is too important to be missed. There are certain things you can only learn about God through suffering. That's what separates the men from the boys." I reflect on my life and the challenges I had to overcome to graduate from ministry school. My first semester, I was pregnant with my first child. Filled with excitement, not realizing that this move was not just for me; it was for four generations of my bloodline. I didn't realize the cost of my *YES*, but I was about to find out. In the first few classes, I felt out of place and lost. I replayed in my mind, "God gives His toughest battles to His strongest soldiers." I didn't give up, even though the opportunities were there. I had so many complications with my pregnancy. My marriage was in turmoil. I had assignments due. Police knocked on my door because my stepdaughter had run away. Then, it was time for me to give birth, and I went through horrifying experiences of postpartum depression. I felt like I could just end it at any moment.

I felt lost because I kept replaying, "Why is God doing this to me? What does He want? Am I alone? Why is everyone else posting up on social media, just living their best lives?" I kept questioning God. Insert eye roll. Yeah, I know you've heard you don't question God, but who's going to give you the answers you need? I had every reason to give up. The opportunity was there to quit. So why did I enroll in the second semester? Like, really?! Did you not see what we went through last semester? Yes, I kept going. No, the trials and tribulations didn't stop, but the rhythm and the frequency changed. It was just like the three Hebrew boys in the fiery furnace. The fire got hotter. The assignments got deeper. The purpose was to transform my thinking.

I had to relearn the things I was taught that I thought were biblical. The cute little Bible stories about creation and Noah and the ark. I was learning on a higher level than what I just repeated from Sunday school lessons during childhood. I experienced my vehicle breaking down. My mom had a stroke. Financial hardships, but this time, I didn't quote "God gives His toughest battles to His strongest soldiers." I started speaking the Word of God over my life.

I found Hebrews 13:5 (AMP), *"Let your character [your moral essence, your inner nature] be free from the love of money [shun greed—be financially ethical], being content with what you have; for He has said, 'I will never [under any circumstances] desert you [nor give you up nor leave you without support, nor will I in any degree leave you helpless], nor will I forsake or let you down or relax My hold on you [assuredly not]!"*

This Scripture shifted my entire being. The attacks intensified during my third and fourth semesters. However, I wasn't the girl in the back of the class who didn't talk because

I felt I didn't belong there and didn't know how to quote Scriptures correctly. I was becoming the woman God called me to be: outspoken, funny, and honest. I wasn't shy. I had legitimately changed the direction of my bloodline. My grandmother would ask me certain things about what I was learning in class, and I would explain it to her. She would always say I was never taught that. I had similar conversations with my mom. My daughter had to be in every class I had, from the beginning to the end. The very foundation of my family shook. Lives had been transformed, and eyes had been opened. We began to see God for who He is: sovereign. That's who He is to us all.

Ultimately, I received an email that altered the trajectory of my life. I had been nominated to speak in front of my class at graduation. That meant I would be standing on the stage alongside a world-renowned bishop, addressing my classmates around the world, from Africa to the big city of Chicago. The enemy pulled out every trick, and I quoted every Scripture I could remember off the top of my head. I even told myself I wasn't worthy of the assignment. It was bigger than me. I silenced the noise of everything falling apart to get there. I stood on that stage and looked at what God did when I started speaking the Word over my life.

I said all that to say this: through Scripture, we must learn to see ourselves as God sees us. He knows the sound of our voices. It's important for us to lean in and study Scripture and remind God of His Word.

> Psalms 119:49-50 (KJV) says, *"Remember the word unto Thy servant, upon which Thou hast caused me to hope. This is my comfort in my affliction: for Thy word hath quickened me."*

The trials I face now are different because of the transformation I went through in my past season. If I had never gone through ministry school, I wouldn't be where I am today. I fight differently. We must break the curses that have been passed down through misquotes and misinformation. Future victories depend on it. Even in our sinful nature, we know right from wrong. We have access to so much information that we have no excuse for being uninformed about the Word. Let's start prioritizing quality alone time with God. Ask God what He's trying to get us to see in these moments of affliction.

When the storms of life become unbearable, remember Ephesians 6:13 (KJV), *"Wherefore take unto you the whole armor of God, that ye may be able to withstand in the evil day, and having done all, to stand."*

God is waiting for us with His arms wide open. He desires to have a relationship with us. 3 John 1:2 (NIV) says,

> *"Beloved, I pray that you may prosper in all things and be in health, just as your soul prospers. This is the will of God for our lives. We aren't in the toughest battle. God has already given us the victory through Jesus Christ."*

CHAPTER 12

God Knows My Heart: Healing from Church Hurt

By: Minister Erin Achane

"I ain't going to church! Everybody in there is fake!" I used to shout it loud and proud. "Walking around quoting Scriptures like they're so perfect, but they are worse than me! All they want is money. Been raising money for a building fund since I was a kid, and still no building, but the Pastor has a new Rolls-Royce. Nah, I'm good. I can pray right here at my house. If you ask me, everybody at that church is a big fat hypocrite. You see me, I don't wanna play with God. I know I'm not gonna stop smoking weed. I plan on smoking tonight when I go to the movies, so why would I ask him for forgiveness when I know I'mma keep doing it? No, I'm not ready to give up smoking, and I'm not ready to give up my freedom. I'm still young and I wanna have fun. I'm saved and that's good enough. God knows my heart."

That was me! I wasn't just mad at church people. I was mad at God, too. And I had convinced myself that being saved was just good enough.

In that season, I had broken up with God. I didn't understand Him, and honestly, I didn't want to. I trusted in him, and he didn't give me what I wanted. He didn't give me what I prayed for. Church had prepared me for the blessings, for the mountaintop moments. But nobody told me what to do in the valley. I didn't know how to get out of the pit! How to get unstuck? When God hit me with a no, I was out! I was not prepared for the real fight, the heartbreak, the betrayal, the loss. I was saved, but had no idea what that truly meant.

When I looked at "church," I didn't see Jesus. I saw judgment. I saw people picking apart my clothes and judging my smeared eyeliner from the party the night before. The deacons whispered to me, "Young lady, you smell like weed." How do you know what weed smells like, Deacon Charles? Constantly pointing out my sins.

Nobody saw my brokenness; they just saw my imperfections. So, I decided church wasn't for me. But somewhere deep down, I knew I needed God. Not "their" God. The real God. And I needed a place where I could worship, grow, and develop a relationship with God without judgment. I needed a safe place to be encouraged, to encourage others, to grow my faith, and not get kicked out or isolated when I made a mistake.

I grew up with a twisted image of Him—not a God of love, but a God to be afraid of. I got "saved" at the age of fourteen because I was terrified of going to hell, not because I truly trusted Jesus as my Lord and Savior. My church was great at getting us young folks in the door and getting us saved. Ok, I'm saved, now what? Growing up Pentecostal, our parents would "catch the Holy Ghost," and they would praise the Lord. They would dance and shout. It was a great time! We saw the outward appearance of being thankful, running, dancing, and falling on the floor. I wanna apologize in advance on behalf of all the 80's babies for mocking y'all, we didn't know the real transformation happened on the inside. The dancing and worshiping were not for show! It was because you were thankful for how far God had brought you. We didn't see the transformation on the inside of you! So, I was expecting my life to be a piece of cake. I was expecting to just catch the Holy Ghost and go to church, and everything would be just fine. I was not prepared for when God's will didn't align with mine.

And then my world shattered.

My three-year-old son was murdered. Poisoned. His innocent eyes—the first time I ever felt unconditional love—closed forever. I was undone. Furious. Bitter. Broken.

Where Were You, God?

I believed in Him, but I no longer believed He was good. I couldn't see the purpose. I couldn't see redemption. All I saw was pain. I viewed it as if God was punishing me directly for working at a strip club while I attended LSU, having a baby out of wedlock, or for taking His Grace for granted. His love was hidden in the Scriptures, and I didn't see it. I had to feel it.

From there, my life spiraled. I was relentlessly stubborn. In my opinion, no one had the authority to tell me how to feel because they didn't experience what I went through. They didn't lose what I lost. I could not be persuaded. I was too broken, too bitter, and too hurt to allow the slightest bit of light to shine in my direction. A few years later, I had another son.

While I was grateful to be a mother again, I was disappointed because I thought having another son would heal my broken heart. But all it did was put a band-aid on an open wound, which led to more bad decisions, more anger, and more bitterness. I had ghosted God, and Satan was having a field day with me.

But Grace Found Me!

It was in a jail cell, isolated and stripped of everything, that I finally cried out. Well, more like screamed out. I didn't know how to pray, I just knew how to hurt. I told God everything: my disappointment, my rage, my guilt, my confusion. I cried until the tear ducts dried up. Then, I did something I never did before. I surrendered. I surrendered my all.

And He answered immediately!

Not with a sermon or lecture. Not with punishment. But with **love**. A whisper in my spirit: He said my name! Satan will always call you by your sin, but God calls you by name!

I braced myself for wrath, but what I got was an ocean of mercy. He poured out His Spirit. He showed me my son, alive, happy, safe with Him in heaven. He also showed me there are consequences to sin, but uses those moments to refine our faith. I saw his Love. He gave me my son! He was a true gift! It was Satan. The real enemy. The Great Deceiver. Roaming the earth like a lion seeking whom it may devour. The real "Opp." Satan's only mission is to kill, steal, and destroy, and his only weapon is deception.

Satan only goes after people who are anointed by God, chosen by God before the foundation of the world. Your anointing is so powerful! And Satan's time is limited. He doesn't waste it unless you threaten his kingdom of darkness. When Satan attacks you in such a way, it doesn't even seem fair, especially when you're young, it's because he knows there is a light in you, even when you don't see it. He will send every form of distraction and discouragement he can use to stop you from fulfilling the purpose God has placed on your life when he formed you. But none of it will work! You may have been down for a season, but the comeback is real! Because when you belong to the Lord of Lords, who can stand against you?!

> *"No weapon that is formed against thee shall prosper; and every tongue that shall rise against thee in judgment thou shalt condemn. This is the heritage of the servants of the Lord, and their righteousness is of me, saith the Lord."*
> *—Isaiah 54:17 KJV*

If God be for you, he is more than the entire world against you.

Moving from Religion to Relationship

That night, I met Jesus for real. Not the "catch the Holy Ghost" Jesus. Not the "you going to hell" Jesus. The Jesus who loved me even when I hated Him.

A shift took place. The Scriptures came to life! I saw a glimpse of Him for the first time! By the revelation of his Holy Spirit, I realized being saved is not enough. It may be enough to get me into heaven, but it's not enough to equip us for life when it starts life'ing. We believe in Jesus, but at the same time, we don't know Jesus for ourselves. I can prove it, when trouble hits our lives, it is not supposed to completely take us out of the fight! It is supposed to bring us to our knees in prayer. In the shift, I came to myself! I realized that I am truly more than a conqueror. It dawned on me that God had never left me, nor did He forsake me. I saw for the first time in my life that He had been there the whole time waiting for me with open arms. I started to believe the words in the book!

We all have to deal with heartbreak. All of us have lost something or someone. Was God punishing me? No. I do know that my faith grew. I know him now because I no longer view death as something that happens to old people; it can happen to young people, too, and I feared for my own soul. I experienced grief at such a young age with my only son that I understood what God must have felt like when he gave his only begotten son. I would say, "Well, you know, Lord, what this feels like. You lost your son, too. But he didn't stay in the grave! And neither will mine!" There is hope in Jesus.

> *"And have you completely forgotten this word of encouragement that addresses you as a father addresses his son? It says, "My son, do not make light of the Lord's discipline, and do not lose heart when he rebukes you, because the Lord disciplines the one he loves, and he chastens everyone he accepts as his son." —Hebrews 12:5-8 NIV*

God is the perfect Father, and because he loves us, he chastens us in order to mold us into what he has envisioned. Belief is only manifested when you act on it. You must act it out in real life! Everything I've been through has made me into who God already knew I would become. I started changing the more I hung out with the Lord. It started showing up in how I treated people, how I treated myself, and how I treated God! Believe that God loves you, indisputably, unequivocally, and unconditionally.

Salvation is the start, not the finish. A relationship is built through prayer, trust, and time.

> *"The Lord has appeared of old to me, saying: "Yes, I have loved you with an everlasting love; Therefore with lovingkindness I have drawn you." —Jeremiah 31:3 NKJV*

No matter how far you think you have fallen, He will never stop loving you. He'll never quit trying to get your attention. Because you belong to Him. And what he decrees and declares will come to pass.

This verse had me in my feelings. The Apostle Paul was really going through something when he wrote this.

> *"For I am persuaded that neither death nor life, nor angels nor principalities nor powers, nor things present nor things to come, nor height nor depth, nor any other created thing, shall be able to separate us from the love of God which is in Christ Jesus our Lord." —Romans 8:38-39 NKJV*

I am persuaded that nothing can separate you from the love of God. Nothing. Paul says if I live or if I die, nothing can separate me from the love of God, which is through Jesus.

The mandate is deeper than just being saved. Jesus told Nicodemus, who was a religious leader and who was desperately and earnestly trying to understand what Jesus was saying:

> *Jesus replied. "I tell you the truth, unless you are born again, you will not see the Kingdom of God." —John 3:3 NLT*

He goes on to say in verse 18, something that really puts our relationship with him in perspective.

> *"There is no judgment against anywho who believes in him. But anyone who does not believe in him has already been judged by not believing in God's one and only Son. And the judgment is based on this fact: God's light came into the world, but people loved darkness more than the light, for their actions were evil. All who do evil hate the light and refuse to go near it for fear their sins will be exposed. But those who do what is right come to the light so others can see that they are doing what God wants. —John 3:18-21 NLT*

As Christians, we accept there is a Jesus, but we don't believe in him. I accepted that Jesus was real, but I did not believe in him, and I didn't believe the words in the Bible were true. Jesus told Nicodemus straight up, If you believe me and you love me, then show it in your actions. If Jesus were around in 2025, he would say, "Be about that life then!" God does know your heart, matter of fact, He is the only one who knows your heart, and He knows the truth. It's full of excuses, the blame game, and pride. We have our very own pity party with just one guest, ourselves! Jesus is saying, Follow me!

No judgment. I was there too! I was afraid to go to church. I thought since they went to church, they were already supposed to be "perfect." I didn't see their humanity, but I expected them to see mine. I would get really upset and show Church folks no grace, and give them no second chances when they made a mistake, but I expected them to show me grace and give me a second chance for my mistakes. I had that "main character energy" where it was the Erin show 24 hours a day. I looked at the folks in the church and compared them to God, which was not fair because all have fallen short. While we all strive to be like God, there is no one like God. I focused on the people in the church because I could not stand to look at His light.

Honestly, it was never about the people in the church. That's just what I told myself. I was afraid and ashamed of what the light would shine on my life. I had done so much. While in college, I worked at a strip club for the whole four years. I have done some things that I'm taking to my grave! Thank God we didn't have Facebook Live in 2004! I knew I was a hot mess, and my filthiness would be exposed in his Great Light. And the guilt of my past sins kept me from feeling worthy of forgiveness. My self-doubt and regret were a stronghold. It kept me from truly surrendering to God.

But when I finally had enough. I made a decision that I couldn't carry it anymore. The day He delivered me, it felt like He had put his arms around me, and I felt safe. The weight was gone. The regret was melting away, and the blame game was finally over. I felt loved. I felt like I was seen. I let it all go. His unfailing love, mercy, kindness, and forgiveness would not allow me to stay in darkness when I finally let His light in. It didn't just shine on my sin, it also shone on His forgiveness and mercy. He took away my sin, and forgave me, but He didn't leave me empty; He gave me an inheritance, hope, and a future.

He just didn't want that for me. He wants that for you, too! He wants to deliver you from the bondage of sin! He wants to heal you! He wants you to rest in him. He wants you to stop doing stuff with your strength and ask for directions before you start the journey. He wants you to stop freaking out every time a storm hits your life because He is sleeping on the boat! He is with you! He has equipped us with every good and perfect gift to fulfil the mission, to accomplish His Will. He already foreknew every obstacle, every roadblock, every setback, and shakeback. He not only knows, He commanded it. He is the Beginning and the End. He is the Sovereign King. And we have a duty to complete the task He has set before us, but we can't accomplish the assignment if we don't understand the mission! We only truly find our real, true, authentic selves when we find Him! Our true identity is rooted in his likeness. So, we must go deeper in his presence and in His Word to know Him for ourselves.

> *"Then God said, 'Let Us make man in Our image, according to Our likeness; let them have dominion over the fish of the sea, over the birds of the air, and over the cattle, over all the earth and over every creeping thing that creeps on the earth.' So God created man in His own image; in the image of God He created him; male and female He created them. Then God blessed them, and God said to them, "Be fruitful and multiply; fill the earth and subdue it; have dominion over the fish of the sea, over the birds of the air, and over every living thing that [h]moves on the earth." —Genesis 1:26-28 NKJV*

And I did not see the whole picture. The Bible is not an easy, read the whole thing on a Saturday night novel with a glass of wine on your patio, kind of book! It's massive and can be quite confusing. So don't try to read the whole thing to say you read it all. Good for you if you read the whole Bible. Do you believe what you've read is the question? Your faith will be tested, to make sure.

The book is alive! It is our faith in Jesus that moves us from just being saved to a real relationship with him.

> *"Take heed that you do not despise one of these little ones, for I say to you that in heaven their angels always see the face of My Father who is in heaven. For the Son of Man has come to save that which was lost."*

> *"What do you think? If a man has a hundred sheep, and one of them goes astray, does he not leave the ninety-nine and go to the mountains to seek the one that is straying? And if he should find it, assuredly, I say to you, he rejoices more over that sheep than over the ninety-nine that did not go astray. Even so it is not the will of your Father who is in heaven that one of these little ones should perish."*
> *—Matthew 18:10-11; 18:12-14 NKJV*

Because he is the Good Shepherd, he will leave the 99 to go all out for that one sheep that was lost. I was that sheep! I was lost. It is not his desire for any of us to perish. He wants all of us to have a relationship with him, but we are running out of time.

But I thank you, Jesus, for coming to get little ole me. From the crawfish and rice fields of South Louisiana! You saved a little Creole, Cajun girl like me! You came and got your lost sheep, honey! He did that! And he changed my whole entire life, way better than what I could ask or think!

> *"For God so loved the world that He gave His only begotten son, that whoever believes in him should not perish but have everlasting life." —John 3:16 NKJV*

The enemy wants to pollute what you believe. And if you believe going to church is a waste of time, then the enemy got your belief. We can't let the fact that our feelings were hurt stop us from going to church. I didn't realize the importance of the church. When done properly, it is supposed to help you grow closer to God by explaining the Word in a way you can receive it. We cannot fight this battle alone. Look at our culture, Satan wants us alone, separated from the rest of the sheep! We must be unified!

The Bible says in Matthew 18:20 (NKJV):

> *"For where two or three are gathered together in My name, I am there in the midst of them."*

Just two or three, the Bible says. Imagine the power of God when you show up and make four! I praise Him at the house, and it's really good. But let me get in the same room with other Believers, our spirits leap! This is why worship is so valuable. You know worship, the part we skip when we do go to church. I would get to church late, right before the preacher preached, and skip the worship. Then I wondered why I was thinking of what I was gonna cook the entire sermon! Worship will get rid of that song that has been playing rent-free in your head all week! Put your thoughts on the Lord and his awesomeness! Think about heaven and God in all His Glory sitting on the throne with all the angels surrounding him, and His train filled the temple! Think about how blessed you are to see another day. Think about how good He has been to you. Worship is the key to the Holy of Holies. Without worship, it is hard for us to receive the word because we are still in our heads and thinking about earthly things and not things eternal. Worship will take you out of your flesh and get you into your spirit.

Humble yourself in His presence, put your back into it, get honest, let those tears fall, don't be ashamed, and ask Him to forgive you. Imagine it's just you and Him! Shut down your flesh and allow your Spirit to go into full turn-up mode. Now, you're ready to receive the message. Open up your Bible and take some notes. Go back and read the Word again for yourself and think about it all day; that's meditating on the Word.

In 2025, we have to stop depending on our grandma, aunties, and uncles to tell us what the Bible says. I didn't realize

I had to seek Him for myself. I broke up with God. I had to make a choice to give us another chance. So, I was not waiting on Him. He was waiting on me. And the more time I made for Him, the more I began to see Him moving supernaturally in my life! It was a game of hide and seek; He would find me and say, "You're it!" Then I would go looking for Him! Each time I look for Him with all my heart, I find Him!

> *"But from there you will seek the LORD your God, and you will find Him if you search for Him with all your heart and all your soul." —Deuteronomy 4:29 NKJV*

In closing, there was a shift where this "church hurt" was birthed. Between the Baby Boomers and Generation Z, the enemy has not only used the world to deceive Believers, but he has also used the church itself to cultivate a generation that is stuck in religion and has no real relationship with God. Sorry to burst your bubble, but there is no perfect church because all churches are filled with imperfect people. I've learned to discern a church by the spiritual fruit it bears, not by the earthly toys it possesses. Is the Glory there? Then that's where I need to be! Church planted a seed in me when I was young, when it gave me the Word, even though I didn't understand it or appreciate it. The thing is, the church plants seeds of the Word in your heart, but it's in your everyday life where that seed will grow. It's that part! It's in the middle of your everyday life, you have to stand on His Word that took root.

We live in a time where we fight so hard to keep the traditions of the church and neglect a spiritual connection with God. We push our members to get people saved, but then forget to mention that it's gonna be a fight and you're gonna need the Holy Spirit to help you! We must get back to discipleship, we must speak in the holy spirit and live by example to build disciples who are separated, holy, and advancing the Kingdom of God. But instead, we give them a scroll of everything they can't do anymore once they get saved. Who wants to follow that? Not this generation, obviously! Instead of telling them what they can't do now that they're saved, we should instead tell them who they are in Christ. We should tell them about the inheritance they received as royal heirs! We should tell them about the power of the blood of Jesus. And how the world didn't give them this gift, and the world can't take it away!

But we don't tell them this! We love to blame phones and technology for why this generation moves the way they do. Totally ignoring the fact that we are the ones who brought them the phones! We gave them everything we didn't have, and we forgot to give them what we did have: respect, integrity, and hard work. My generation messed these kids up when we stopped giving them Jesus. We hated the struggle so much when we were young, but we didn't know that the struggle was what made us strong. Have mercy on us, Father! We know not.

We live in a culture that loves the idea of God, loves the daily affirmations, and loves to post a quick AI-generated Scripture on our reels, and we think in doing so, that we have a relationship with God.

> *"You've been had. You've been took. You've been hoodwinked, bamboozled, led astray, run amok. This is what he does."*
> —Denzel Washington in Malcolm X

The Holy Spirit showed me the temperature of our current culture, "A people that has a form of godliness but lacks the power thereof because we refuse to surrender, we refuse to unite and we refuse to repent." We will not accept the possibility that maybe we got it wrong!

We have to check our pride! That's what got Satan caught up! He was evicted from Heaven, you know. Jesus said he saw Satan fall from heaven like lightning to the ground in Luke 10:18-19. (NKJV)

Who can stand against the Army of the Lord?

I'll close with this. Everything on earth is temporary. The comfort, the clout, the cash, the applause, it's all fading faster than ever. People switch up, feelings change, but God stays the same. His love never expires, and His grace doesn't run out. So let it go, the pain, the offense, the shame. Forgive them and then forgive yourself. Ask the Father to forgive you, too, because He is not just the God who sees, He's the God who saves. He will wash you, make you white as snow, fill you with His Holy Spirit, and give you peace in the middle of the storm, and they don't sell that at the mall. He'll give you joy that's not surface-level, but unspeakable, overflowing joy. God wants to heal that church hurt, the one that's been wounded by people but still longs for a real connection with Him. And yes, He knows your heart. He knows the hurt behind your habits, the fear beneath your independence, the broken pieces you don't show anyone, and He loves you anyway. But stop using "God knows my heart" as a reason to stay away.

> *"Behold, the days come, saith the Lord God, that I will send a famine in the land, not a famine of bread... but of hearing the words of the Lord." —Amos 8:11–12 KJV*

"But know this, that if the master of the house had known what hour the thief would come, he would have watched and not allowed his house to be broken into. Therefore you also be ready, for the Son of Man is coming at an hour you do not expect." —Luke 12:39-40 NKJV

"And then the lawless one will be revealed,
whom the Lord will consume with the breath of His mouth and destroy with the brightness of His coming. The coming of the lawless one is according to the working of Satan,
with all power, signs, and lying wonders, and with all unrighteous deception among those who perish, because they did not receive the love of the truth, that they might be saved.
And for this reason God will send them strong delusion,
that they should believe the lie, that they all may be condemned who did not believe the truth but had pleasure in unrighteousness."
—2 Thessalonians 2:8-12 NKJV

CHAPTER 13

I'mma Just Wait On GOD

By: Minister Herbert Poole

"Wait on the LORD: be of good courage,
and he shall strengthen thine heart: wait, I say, on the LORD."
—Psalm 27:14 KJV

David faced many challenges as a son, shepherd, apprentice, soldier, husband, father, and king. While the specific circumstances he found himself in when writing this Psalm are not clearly known, one thing is very clear throughout most of his life. He was a man who trusted and waited on God.

Waiting may sound passive. But it requires faith, trust, and, more often, some action on our part. Whether carrying on with life while believing God to fulfil a promise, like Abraham and Sarah. Or standing still and waiting on God to move like Moses and the children of Israel as they stood on the banks of the Red Sea being pursued by Pharaoh's armies.

Have there been instances in your life when, in retrospect, you wished you'd spoken up about something? Maybe it was a situation where you could have defended yourself or someone else. A circumstance where you were mistreated or didn't receive what you deserved. A scenario where the powers that be didn't consider you while accommodations were being made for others.

Ecclesiastes 3:1-8 says (NIV):

> 1 *There is a time for everything,*
> *and a season for every activity under the heavens:*
> 2 a time to be born and a time to die,
> *a time to plant and a time to uproot,*
> 3 a time to kill and a time to heal,
> *a time to tear down and a time to build,*
> 4 a time to weep and a time to laugh,
> *a time to mourn and a time to dance,*
> 5 a time to scatter stones and a time to gather them,
> *a time to embrace and a time to refrain from embracing,*
> 6 a time to search and a time to give up,
> *a time to keep and a time to throw away,*
> 7 a time to tear and a time to mend,
> *a time to be silent and a time to speak,*
> 8 a time to love and a time to hate,
> *a time for war and a time for peace.*

I'd like to draw your attention to the latter part of verse 7. It states, "There is a time to be silent." But it goes on to also say, "There is a time to speak."

One of the biggest challenges is discerning the appropriate time for each. This can be particularly challenging when it comes to confronting what has already been established or set in motion, perhaps when the circumstances appear to dictate that it's not your place to say something.

This is precisely the situation that Mahlah, Noah, Hoglah, Milcah, and Tirzah found themselves in as Moses and the leadership of Israel prepared to distribute the land they were about to possess. These women are the daughters of Zelophehad, an Israelite who died in the wilderness and had no sons to receive his inheritance.

There are many times when we take the position that if God intends for it to be, He will make it happen. I mean, He is all-knowing, right? Why wouldn't He have considered a situation like this and already made provision for them? Moses, the elders? Had no one else thought about this? Maybe it had been discussed and decided.

I remember hearing these words of wisdom at some point during my childhood. "The answer is always no until you ask!" Albeit no matter how profound, all too often, I've reasoned within myself as to why it was better or safer to remain silent. Whether it was apathy, low self-esteem, or fear, I chose to go with the flow. As the old saying goes, "Que sera, sera!"

I am the secondborn of my mother's four children. I am also the only male. My three sisters each have very unique personalities. I can imagine these five sisters discussing this situation among themselves. Some were probably more concerned than others regarding the predicament they found themselves in. Perhaps it was a bit of a taboo subject. I'd venture to guess there may have been at least one sister who preferred not to "rock the boat," so to speak. Did they hold a vote? Did they confer with anyone outside their immediate family? Had anyone else encouraged them to speak up? How would the rest of the Israelites view them?

When I think of this group of women and their boldness, I can't help but think of my youngest sister. Her boldness often inspires and challenges me. I could very well see her leading the charge in a situation like this. Though the youngest, she'd most likely be the spokesperson for the family. I've witnessed

God work and move on her behalf over the years in amazing and similar ways.

How many times do we say we're just waiting on God? Truth be told, He is more often waiting on us. In Matthew 7:7, Jesus gives the admonition to ask, seek, and knock. These are actions that He says will precipitate a response.

> *"Ask, and it shall be given you; seek, and ye shall find; knock, and it shall be opened to you." —Matthew 7:7 KJV*

When it came time for the children of Israel to possess the promised land, God didn't just snap His fingers and wipe out all the existing inhabitants. They had an active role to play. Even at times when God literally fought for them, they still had to remain engaged and follow the instructions they were given to carry out.

Remember Queen Esther? She finds favor with King Ahasuerus at a time when a devious plot is unfolding to have the Jews exterminated. She has a choice to make. Will she remain silent and play it safe? Or will she risk her life to preserve the lives of her people? Her cousin, Mordecai, tells her, "Do not think that because you are in the king's house you alone of all the Jews will escape. For if you remain silent at this time, relief and deliverance for the Jews will arise from another place, but you and your father's family will perish. And who knows but that you have come to your royal position for such a time as this?"

We often think of the fact that our actions have consequences. But how frequently do we consider the same when it comes to our inaction? Depending upon the circumstances of a situation, our lack of action can be just as devastating.

> *"The only thing necessary for the triumph of evil is that good men do nothing."*
> – Edmund Burke

In 1 Samuel 30, we see King David at one of his lowest points. He and his men have returned to their camp only to find that it has been raided, and their women and children have been taken. His men are so distraught that they are ready to stone him. But he begins to encourage himself and has the wisdom to inquire of God to see if they should pursue those who have perpetrated this evil against them. In his grief and despair, King David could have sat in silence, accepted defeat, and whatever fate lay before him. This paid off in a huge victory, as God told him to pursue this enemy and that they would recover all. They did just that!

There were several times, as my mother's health began to decline, that I felt prompted to call and have someone check on her. These instances led to her being taken to the hospital, where she received lifesaving treatment. Had she not received the medical care that was needed in these situations, she wouldn't have remained with us as long as she did. I could have just prayed and said, "It's all in God's hands."

In 1 Corinthians 3:9, Scripture tells us that we are laborers together with God. That will look somewhat different for each of us. We all have our spheres of influence. Our favor and boldness, presence in various times and places, wisdom and discernment. All these factors play an important role.

Even as we read the great examples of those who have come before us, we are tremendously gifted with the presence of the

Holy Spirit. He leads us into truth, teaches us, and empowers us. We are called to be ambassadors for Christ and agents of positive change to our generation.

In Acts 4, following the death, burial, and resurrection of Jesus, we see John and Peter being brought before the leaders of their day. They are questioned and threatened, told to no longer speak or teach in the name of JESUS. In response, they pray the following prayer:

> *"Now, Lord, consider their threats and enable your servants to speak your word with great boldness." —Acts 4:29 NIV*

We can't change the past. But we can learn from it and grow. What is God challenging you to step up to the plate for? Where has He given you a voice, platform, and influence to make a difference? If you don't know, ask Him today. Your choices have eternal consequences and affect the trajectory of your life as well as the lives of those connected to you. Don't miss your shot!

Conclusion

Chapter by chapter, page by page, we have exposed the enemy, uprooted deception, and reminded you of the authority you carry when you stand on the Kingdom of God. Every phrase the world has twisted, every lie we've adopted, every slogan we've spiritualized without Scripture—those strongholds are being torn down in Jesus' name.

Why? Because the anointing breaks every yoke.

The yoke of false doctrine? Broken.

The yoke of fear and anxiety? Broken.

The yoke of comparison, compromise, and complacency? Broken.

The yoke of poverty, addiction, generational curses, trauma, rejection, and shame? Broken.

Not by our power. Not by our intellect. Not by our titles or talents.

But by the anointing of the Holy Spirit.

This book was written in the anointing. And that same anointing is now resting on you.

You've been awakened. You've been equipped. And now it's time to act.

The veil has been lifted.

What culture tried to camouflage, the Spirit has now uncovered.

The Kingdom is no longer hidden—it's being revealed.

The Kingdom of God is rising in the hearts of those who will not be silenced, diluted, or deceived.

The enemy can no longer hide behind half-truths and cute captions. The Spirit of the Lord is upon us, and He has anointed us to preach the good news, to set captives free, to open blind eyes, and to proclaim the acceptable year of the Lord.

So now, we charge you:

Speak boldly.

Stand firmly.

Pray deeply.

Move obediently.

Worship freely.

Serve faithfully.

Love radically.

You were born for this moment. You were handpicked for this fight. God is not surprised by the times we're living in, and He's not intimidated by them either. He placed you here, in this generation, for a divine purpose:

Not to blend in. Not to bow down.

You are not alone. You are part of a remnant rising. A generation that will fight back in the Spirit. A people who will not fold. A remnant that cannot be silenced.

The Kingdom suffers violence, and the violent take it by force (Matthew 11:12).

You were called to be a light in the middle of confusion. You were called to speak the truth in the face of compromise. You were called to war — not against people, but against lies and deception, against anything that tries to exalt itself above the knowledge of God. *"For the weapons of our warfare are not carnal but mighty in God for pulling down strongholds, casting down arguments and every high thing that exalts itself against the knowledge of God."* (2 Corinthians 10:4-5 NKJV)

This book is your training ground. This book is a reminder that you don't have to stay stuck.

You don't have to live lukewarm. You don't have to settle for quotes when you are called to walk in Kingdom authority. You have the power to discern. You have the power to overcome. You have the power to fight back!

Lay down the slogans. Pick up your sword.

Refuse to be another Believer who knows how to post Scriptures but doesn't know how to live them. Refuse to be another Christian that Satan laughs at because you know the memes but not the manual.

This is your call to spiritual maturity and authority.

This is your call to wake up.

The Kingdom needs you. This next generation needs you. The battle is already raging, and silence is no longer an option.

Because **Satan is your Opp**.

But God is your victory.

So, step forward.

Stand up.

Speak out.

Welcome to the movement.

Welcome to the fight.

Welcome to the Kingdom.

About the Authors

Patsy Hill is a devoted minister with a passion for training and equipping others for Kingdom living. She has been joyfully married to her husband, Jerry, for 38 years. Together, they have been blessed with four wonderful children, three sons and one daughter, and four cherished grandchildren. In addition to her ministry, Patsy is a registered nurse who enjoys reading, fishing, and crafting in her free time. She currently resides in Killeen, Texas.

Erin Achane is a spirit-led minister and a passionate multi-business owner. Born and raised in Crowley, LA, Erin has been married to her husband for 11 beautiful years, and together they are raising four incredible children—including a set of twins—with faith, love, and purpose. Erin's mission is clear: to see people, especially the next generation, stand boldly on the Kingdom of God. #SOK

Herbert Poole is a man of great compassion with a heart and mission to see others experience the life-changing love of GOD that has so radically transformed his life. Born and raised in Chicago, Illinois. He now resides in Houston, Texas, with his wife of 32 years. He's a father to three grown children and a grandfather to fourteen grandchildren. He has been a software developer for over 20 years. Herbert also writes poetry, sings, and is learning to play acoustic guitar. He often shares his poetry online using the handle "Scribe of Judah" or @ scribeofjudah.

Jeanette Lebron grew up in Elizabeth, New Jersey, and has dedicated her life to serving both her community and the Kingdom of God. She is an elder and worship leader at her local church, where her passion for ministry and people shines through. With a background in public administration, Jeanette brings years of experience in leadership and service to every role she undertakes. Her heart for people, worship, and purposeful living is the foundation of everything she does.

Ron Campbell, nurtured in Houston, TX, grew up serving my immediate community with the gifts that God gave. Adventurer, I'm fascinated with the outdoors and what it reveals. My earliest years were spent in church choir, Bible studies, church plays, etc. Background in the oil and gas industry for over 20 years. Father, grandfather, and a man of God. I hope to be all that He has called me to be. My daily inspection appears on YouTube @RoseBlue2024.

John Drew Davidson Jr. was born in Buffalo, NY, and raised in New Orleans, LA, from the age of 5 up to 18 when Hurricane Katrina hit, causing John and his family to relocate back to Buffalo. There he met his wife, Charlette, and they have been together for 17 years, raising three beautiful daughters. John likes to play basketball, cook, and draw/paint whenever he has spare time (which is never). To encourage and enlighten people with the living Word of God is John's purpose on earth, and his ministry can be found on social media platforms @ sonofdavidmessages and on YouTube at "Son of David Messages".

Priscilla Jones is a minister, creative designer, and entrepreneur. She has cultured relationships with many people from different backgrounds. She has spoken truth, motivation, and inspired people from all over the world. She is a phenomenal wife and mother to two beautiful children. She loves to write, sing, and encourage others. Her motto is: Grace changes everything.

Jacquelyn Jones is a woman of faith, purpose, and resilience, a modern-day "Sarah" known for bold prayers and unwavering trust in God. Born in Tennessee and raised in Wisconsin, she now lives in Fort Worth, Texas, with her loving husband, Donald. Together, they've blended a family of five children, 2 sons-in-law, and 1 daughter-in-law—including two who have passed—15 grandchildren, and 14 great-grandchildren, with heartfelt remembrance of a grandson and great-grandson now with the Lord. A licensed minister, intercessor, and outreach worker, Jacquelyn is devoted to restoration and biblical truth. She is also a first-time author, recording artist, and entrepreneur. Her ministry flows through worship, teaching, and songwriting. In her spare time, she enjoys sewing, reading, walking, baseball, and sharing laughter with loved ones.

For more information, click the QR code.

www.ministersinaction.com

www.ingramcontent.com/pod-product-compliance
Lightning Source LLC
Chambersburg PA
CBHW070753100426
42742CB00012B/2118